Educational
Media
Selection Centers

ALA Studies in Librarianship

Number 1

Educational Media Selection Centers

IDENTIFICATION AND ANALYSIS OF CURRENT PRACTICES

JOHN ROWELL
Project Director
Case Western Reserve University

and

M. ANN HEIDBREDER
Project Coordinator
National Book Committee

AMERICAN LIBRARY ASSOCIATION

CHICAGO 1971

The research reported herein was performed pursuant to a contract with the Office of Education, U.S. Department of Health, Education, and Welfare. Contractors undertaking such projects under government sponsorship are encouraged to express freely their professional judgment in the conduct of the project. Points of view or opinions stated do not, therefore, necessarily represent official Office of Education position or policy.

The final report for the Educational Media Selection Centers Project, Phase I, was submitted by the National Book Committee to the Office of Education under the title of THE ORGANIZATION AND OPERATION OF EDUCATIONAL MEDIA SELECTION CENTERS: Identification and Analysis of Current Practices and Guidelines for Model Centers. The Project Number is 8-0515. The Educational Document Number in the ERIC system is ED 036201.

International Standard Book Number 0-8389-0088-7 (1971)
Library of Congress Catalog Card Number 75-140213
Printed in the United States of America

Contents

Preface
and
Acknowledgments

A project of the scope of <u>Educational Media Selection</u>
<u>Centers: Identification and Analysis of Current Practices</u>
requires the talents and teamwork of numerous people and
the cooperation and resources of a variety of organizations
and agencies. The operation of this study demonstrated the
potential of the current trend to draw on the expertise of both
public and private agencies for the common benefit of each
sector. The principal agencies participating in Phase I were
the National Book Committee, the U.S. Office of Education,
the Center for Documentation and Communication Research
of Case Western Reserve University; the institutions and
organizations represented on the Executive Advisory Council
and those on the larger Advisory Committee, its successor,
served as advisors to the project.

Time after time I was impressed and encouraged by the
eagerness of the individual agency in the educational establishment to break new ground; to help find new patterns of
media selection, organization, and function; and to share its
strengths and question its own limitations. The nearly 2,000
individuals who took the time to answer questionnaires, to
reply to letters, and to involve untold others on their staffs
and in their agencies have earned the respect and gratitude
of all who were responsible for the management of this project. In addition, several hundred others willingly served on
on-site visit teams, opened their centers to the team visitors,
participated in long sessions of briefing and debriefing, and
shared their accumulated information and professional judgment with the project's staff and consultants. We are deeply
grateful to all for the goodwill they have generated for the
project, as well as for their professional competence, their
willingness to accept and meet short deadlines, travel long
distances, and write reports.

During the course of Phase I of the project we saw the concept of the educational media selection center being transformed from one of a depository center orientation to one of a service function orientation. Repeatedly, participants in the project expressed a readiness to learn from one another in the process of discovering; this was reflected in reports of the constant growth and change in concepts and definitions of progress, service, and administrative techniques in the centers themselves. Begun as an information-gathering study, Phase I of the project often has become a catalyst for action within the centers.

Beyond this, for me personally the experience of working on this project has afforded a unique opportunity to see the relationships between the many aspects of the education and library professions and allied and supporting industries and organizations. As director of this project, working with a variety of leading educators, librarians, and other professions in a new context - not as a professor or a librarian or an officer of a professional organization - I have seen the vitality and essentiality of productive interdependence. In 1969 the American Association of School Librarians (ALA) and the Department of Audio Visual Instruction (NEA) jointly published the new national Standards for School Media Programs; this interdependence of concerned groups is imperative if the Standards are to make their guiding impact in the fields of educational excellence. New users of instructional media programs have been identified; new patterns of organization are required; new kinds and new mixes of professional and supportive competence are emerging.

One component in the instructional landscape of the 1970s, and we believe it to be an important one, is the educational media selection center function. We discovered a very great degree of willing flexibility of people to cope with demands and changes in the concept of the selection center function. Their participation in Phase I of this project suggests a positive future for the implementation of the Standards.

A number of people in demanding professional positions have made exceptional contributions to the development of Phase I. In addition to the pressures of their other responsibilities, they have sustained directorial and consultative guidance. Chief among them was M. Ann Heidbreder, Staff Associate of the National Book Committee, Inc., and Project Coordinator.

Special appreciation is also extended to Dr. Frances Henne and Mr. A. Edward Miller of the Executive Advisory Council and to those other members of the Advisory Committee who served on visiting teams, tested the sample instruments, and gave frequent and invaluable consultant services. Grateful recognition is also made of the high performance research assistance provided by Miss Mary Virginia Gaver of Rutgers - The State University of New Jersey and by Dr. Milton L. Blum, consulting psychologist. The editorial contribution of Miss Patricia Preuss was most valuable.

Finally, we wish to acknowledge what we consider an especially significant opportunity afforded by the Office of Education's Bureau of Research. It is not often that studies funded by a research agency can show immediate results. We have evidence that this one already has done so. We have learned that leadership by people of commitment works where people care to make it work. In a decade when young people are being educated at all times in all places, all kinds of people contribute to their education. We have discovered that these educators, professional and informal, do make use of the materials and functions of media selection centers to improve the quality of the educational process. We have learned that they consider the functions of the centers essential to their own work and that they are pressing for the further development of these services. We have also learned that in some small ways in some districts, the very self-evaluation and inventory of purpose imposed on the resident staffs as a part of this project have resulted in new and closer relationships between librarians and audiovisual specialists and between the centers' staffs and their administrators and their users.

Working from the base of experience discovered in Phase I and outlined in this report, the educational media selection center project staff and committees are eager to commence the next steps in Phase II. I offer every good wish to my successor, Cora Paul Bomar.

John Rowell,
Project Director

Case Western Reserve University
Cleveland, Ohio
January 1970

1
Introduction

SUMMARY OF PHASE I

SUMMARY OF PHASE I

In the eighteen months allotted for that purpose, the
National Book Committee has completed Phase I of this
project, the aim of which has been to contribute to the development of quality education by improving the selection and
use of educational media. During this phase the project has
surveyed facilities and examined programs which introduce
teachers, librarians, and other concerned professional
adults to the wide range of media that exist at the state,
regional, and local levels, to support and supplement education. When such facilities and programs were located and
identified, the successful components were evaluated. Two
questionnaires were mailed - the first to all known facilities,
the second to 440 identified centers - and on the basis of the
findings, 38 centers were selected for on-site evaluation by
teams of at least two, and in most cases three, professionals.
The team reports were analyzed and tabulated; and, for the
purpose of validating the findings, those of the team members
who were able to give the time attended additional group discussion sessions. Much information of value in the writing
of the "Guide" (Phase II) for educational media selection centers was elicited during Phase I.

The primary purpose of the first questionnaire was to determine whether or not the respondent offered one or more
aspects of an educational media selection center program.
Ideally, such a center is a place which houses a wide variety
of media and which conducts a full-scale training program in
the techniques of selecting and using media for librarians,
teachers, educational supervisory personnel, and other adults.
The media in these centers are professionally evaluated and
purchased. Various other services (in-service guidance, dynamics of utilization of media in schools, identification of

sources of materials and procedures for acquisition) are offered.

Although the first mailing (1, 995) generated an unusually high percentage of response (79%), only 440 of these respondents received the second comprehensive questionnaire requesting specific information about the nature and size of media and equipment collections, sources of funds, staffing patterns, and services or programs offered. Two hundred and twelve of the responses to the second questionnaire exhibited valid media selection center components; these were tabulated and analyzed for this report.

The major objective of both instruments was to help determine which centers were to receive on-site surveys. One research technique introduced in this study and not widely used, if used before at all in library research, was that of holding group discussion sessions for the team members after their visits for further evaluation.

The findings, based on the questionnaires and team evaluations, are that very few educational media selection centers exist as originally described. There is, however, a pressing need for the establishment of media selection centers. Many of the important functions previously described are being carried out in local and state school systems primarily, in varying degrees of effectiveness. The differences among such places and programs are much more apparent than the similarities. Perhaps the most optimistic finding is the high degree of support on the part of center staff and users for educational media selection centers. Among the more serious problems are the separation of print and nonprint media and services in many places, the lack of capability to conduct continuing, professional in-service training programs, and the limitations on continuous funding for centers. Of great concern is the need to motivate teachers, librarians, administrators, and other concerned adults to learn about the wealth of educational media that is available and about ways to use it in the educational process. The identification of centers in top and bottom thirds was confirmed by the judgment of team evaluations and also by the interviews.

The first and fundamental recommendation is that the "Guide to the Development of Educational Media Selection Centers" be written and disseminated as widely as possible, with recommendations for its implementation. Educators in general and media specialists/librarians in particular not only realize the need for improving the selection and use of media, they also consider educational media selection centers to be vital to this process. The proposed "Guide" can help at two levels - (1) to define the philosophy and role of such centers in the total education process; (2) to make specific recommendations about staff, facilities, media collections in centers, education programs, and communication with users of centers, including administrators.

The second recommendation for the project is that several model or demonstration centers be established in a variety of administrative patterns (school system, public library system, college or university) across the country so that interested educators could visit one or more nearby centers to learn how such facilities can be operated for the benefit of all concerned adults and ultimately, of course, for the nation's children and young adults.

DEVELOPMENT OF THE PROGRAM

Identifying the Need

Some of the most thoughtful and respected leaders of American education have stated that a major goal of education must be to help children learn to use a wide range of educational tools. However, despite accelerated publication and production of a variety of instructional media, millions of children still do not have access to these important educational tools.

Far too many teachers and other adults, professional and paraprofessional, who work with children are unaware that there exist media appropriate to curriculum and especially geared to children's needs and interests. In addition, many educators are not only unable to judge media, they are also unable to use them effectively with children, probably because the majority of teacher education institutions have not been and are not now providing adequate instruction in the selection and use of educational media. One medium, children's trade books, points up the magnitude of the problem with which many bewildered and helpless educators are confronted - the more than 3, 000 children's books published each year. Even in schools where media properly organized for use are provided, most teachers have little or no opportunity either to find out

3

what is available or to learn how to make effective use of
these materials in the classroom.

In the past, the textbook was the primary, and often the
sole, teaching tool; today the textbook can be supplemented by
a wide variety of media, in many kinds of formats, to motivate children and young adults. Among such media are books,
periodicals, documents, pamphlets, photographs, reproduc-
tions, pictorial or graphic works, musical scores, maps,
charts, globes, sound recordings (including but not limited to
those on discs and tapes), processed slides, transparencies,
films, filmstrips, kinescopes, and video tapes. Yet not all
teachers and students are benefiting from the various high
quality educational media available. Children are being taught
how to read (though not with universal effectiveness, as U.S.
Commissioner of Education James Allen stressed in his "Right
to Read" speech in September 1969), but too few educational
systems are offering children a real range of materials to
read after they have mastered the basic skills. Similarly, the
visual, auditory, and tactile learning resources have not been
exploited to an extent commensurate with their educational
importance and potential, largely because those who are in a
position to select, purchase, and use media rarely have access
to a comprehensive, current collection for examination and
comparison.

A partial and effective solution to this last problem lies in
professionally conducted, community-based training programs
for in-service teachers, librarians, audiovisual specialists,
curriculum supervisors, and other adults (both inside and out-
side the formal school system). A wide variety and number of
appropriate media must support such instruction so that the
in-service trainee can examine and evaluate the collections
available before attempting to introduce them in the classroom.
For the purposes of this study, such places where this instruction took place were identified as educational media
selection centers. The function and responsibility of the
center were conceived to be (1) a comprehensive collection of
teaching and learning resources which serves as a depository
for examination and selection, and (2) a place where in-service
training programs are conducted.

Librarians, information scientists, and media specialists
traditionally have been responsible for the evaluation and
selection of all types of materials, and are now assuming an
increasing responsibility for training teachers and other adults

4

to use media with students. This instructional leadership is, however, handicapped by a shortage of library and information science manpower. Given the quantity and range of material that now exists, coupled with this critical shortage of trained specialists, it will be virtually impossible in the future to staff individual schools with highly skilled specialists. Therefore, it is essential that a coordinated effort be made now to establish centralized centers, where highly skilled media specialists can maximize their effectiveness.

The existence of such media centers should have a substantive effect on the quality of education for all students, but especially so for one specific target population, the educationally disadvantaged child. Many teachers and other professionals who work with these children are unaware of the existence of media that would help them reach and motivate these children, especially those at the preschool and primary levels. In the past five years especially, it has been charged that materials for disadvantaged children could not be found. In reality such children have not had access to existing materials because (1) the schools they attended either had inadequate libraries or none at all, or (2) in some states and counties "integrated" materials or materials about ethnic groups had not been approved for purchase. Where attempts have been made to create special materials, these too often have been inferior and decidedly inappropriate in their flavor and content. For example, a three-year-old black child does not need a specially written ABC book; he does need the very best and most appealing ABC book available. By collecting all appropriate, current materials in media selection centers, the staff can introduce teachers, public and school librarians, paraprofessionals, day-care and youth workers to the wealth of preschool material that does exist.

Where it has often been impractical for teachers to be released from their classrooms for extended periods of time for prolonged in-service training or other advanced professional courses, the media center would offer convenient and immediate help with specific problems. Full and frequent use of the center's program and resources could provide any teacher with continuing professional development and upgrading, stimulation, and new ideas and techniques.

5

Role of the National Book Committee

The National Book Committee,[1] which has made a number of other studies on the innovative use of books and related media (for example, a survey of "Neighborhood Library Centers and Services" for the Office of Economic Opportunity), undertook the present study with the conviction that it would have far-reaching effects on the learning process, thus encouraging educational excellence.

The objectives for Phase I were determined to be the following:

> To establish advisory and administrative operations for the project
>
> To develop a questionnaire that would identify existing educational media selection centers in the United States
>
> To evaluate the centers so identified and to select those centers or programs which, in one or more aspects, were performing at a level justifying further research
>
> To develop a second, more comprehensive, questionnaire with which to study those centers or programs selected after evaluating the data supplied by the first questionnaire for the purpose of identifying components of strengths and weaknesses of these centers as related to their operation and effectiveness
>
> To direct on-site visits by teams to a sample of centers selected from evaluations of the data of the two questionnaires
>
> To gather information from the on-site visiting teams for the final report on Phase I, preparatory to the development and drafting of the "Guide to the Development of Educational Media Selection Centers" (Phase II).

Role of the Advisors

Phase I of the project was divided into four major activity areas - creation and analysis of the first questionnaire; crea-

---

1. The National Book Committee was established in 1954 as a nonprofit membership corporation of prominent citizens representing education, the arts and sciences, communications, business, and the professions. It has been responsible for several conferences, research projects and publications, and public information, reading, and library development programs.

tion and analysis of the second questionnaire; the visits of on-site survey teams to centers demonstrating elements of the ideal media selection center program; analysis and evaluation of these elements in this report.

To provide expert guidance for the project, the National Book Committee in the summer of 1968 invited leaders in the education, library, and information science fields to serve on the Executive Advisory Council. They are:

Chairman: Dr. Mason W. Gross, President, Rutgers - The State University, New Jersey

Miss Elenora Alexander, Director of Instructional Materials Services, Houston Independent School District

Mr. Arthur Brody, President and General Manager, Bro-Dart Industries

Dr. O. L. Davis, Jr., Associate Professor, Curriculum and Instruction, University of Texas, Austin

Dr. Robert Gerletti, Director, Division of Educational Media, Los Angeles County Schools

Mr. Alvin Goldwyn, Director, Center for Documentation and Communication Research, Case Western Reserve University

Dr. Frances Henne, Professor, Columbia University, School of Library Service, New York City

Mrs. Mary F. K. Johnson, School of Education, University of North Carolina at Greensboro

Dr. Carl L. Marburger, Commissioner of Education, State Department of Education, New Jersey

The Most Reverend John B. McDowell, Auxiliary Bishop of Pittsburgh, Catholic Schools Office

Mr. A. Edward Miller, President, Berlitz Publications, Inc., and former president of Alfred Politz Research

Dr. Franklin Patterson, President, Hamshire College, Amherst, Massachusetts

Mr. Harold Tucker, Librarian, Queens Borough Public Library

Mr. Theodore Waller, President, Grolier Educational Corporation and a member of the Executive Committee of the National Book Committee and of the Executive Committee of the American Book Publishers Council

To assure an even wider range of professional guidance for the completion of Phase I and to help plan and implement the subsequent phases of the program, a larger, more broadly representative Advisory Committee was formed. The Advisory Committee, which has absorbed the original Executive Advisory Council, with Dr. Gross continuing as chairman of the expanded group, held its first meeting in the fall of 1969. Following are the new members of the Advisory Committee and the organizations which they represent.[2]

Dr. Dorothy M. McGeoch,
American Association of Colleges for Teacher Education
Mr. Roger Yarrington,
American Association of Junior Colleges
Mr. Arnold W. Salisbury,
American Association of School Administrators
Miss Leila Doyle,
American Association of School Librarians
Mr. Sanford Cobb,
American Book Publishers Council
Dr. John Caffrey,
American Council on Education
Mr. Francis S. Fox,
American Educational Publishers Institute
Mr. David Selden,
American Federation of Teachers
Miss Mary V. Gaver
American Library Association
Mr. David Shaw
American Institute of Architects
Dr. Merle M. Ohlsen,
American Personnel & Guidance Association
Mr. Joseph Becker,
American Society for Information Science
Dr. Sue Arbuthnot,
Association for Childhood Education International
Miss Erma R. Schell,
Association of Classroom Teachers
Mr. Philip J. McNiff,
Association of College and Research Libraries
Dr. Ralph Van Dusseldorp,
Association for Educational Data Systems

2. Refer to the Executive Advisory Council list to complete the Advisory Committee roster.

Dr. Ridgley M. Bogg,
Association of School Business Officials
Mr. James S. Cookston,
Association of State School Library Supervisors
Dr. Alexander Frazier,
Association for Supervision and Curriculum Development
Sister Helen Sheehan,
Catholic Library Association
Mr. Robert Verrone,
Children's Book Council
Dr. Carl L. Marburger,
Council of Chief State School Officers
Mr. Lee E. Campion,
Department of Audiovisual Instruction
Dr. Howard Hitchens, Jr.,
Department of Audiovisual Instruction
Mr. John D. Greene,
Department of Elementary-Kindergarten-Nursery
Education
Mr. Andrew J. Mitchell,
Department of Elementary School Principals
Mr. Gordon I. Swanson,
Department of Rural Education
Dr. Helen Huus,
International Reading Association
Mr. William G. Harley
National Association of Educational Broadcasters
Mr. Cary Potter,
National Association of Independent Schools
Mr. Curtis Johnson,
National Association of Secondary School Principals
Mr. John C. Ellingson,
National Audio-Visual Association, Inc.
Rev. C. Albert Koob,
The National Catholic Education Association
Mr. Gerald E. Sroufe,
National Committee for Support of the Public Schools
Mrs. Irvin E. Hendryson,
National Congress of Parents and Teachers
Dr. Ralph W. Cordier,
National Council for the Social Studies
Mr. William A. Jenkins,
National Council of Teachers of English

Dr. Julius H. Hlavaty,
The National Council of Teachers of Mathematics

Senior Resident Consultants for Phase I were Peter S. Jennison, executive director, and Virginia H. Mathews, staff associate, of the National Book Committee.

METHODOLOGY AND PROCEDURES

The method of gathering data was designed not only to obtain information but also to allow for the evolving of objective procedures for interpreting the data gathered. The research design can be broken down into thirteen stages:

1. Initial identification of agencies indicating one or more components of an educational media selection center program selected from eleven public and private sources
2. A sample first questionnaire, tested in Florida and Pennsylvania
3. A revised first questionnaire, mailed to facilities in the remaining 48 states and U.S. dependent territories (see Appendix A)
4. An analysis of the first questionnaire from a summary tabulation of the agencies evidencing one or more components of an educational media selection center (see "Mail Questionnaire Surveys," p. 19-22)
5. A sample second questionnaire, designed to elicit a more precise profile of the facility to be surveyed, also tested in Florida and Pennsylvania
6. A revised second questionnaire, mailed to the remaining agencies not eliminated in the analysis of the first questionnaire (see Appendix B)
7. An analysis from the summary tabulation of the returns (see p. 19-25, "Mail Questionnaire Surveys")
8. Preparation and production of questionnaire interview forms for the use of on-site survey teams (see Appendixes C and D)
9. On-site visits conducted in 38 places in 22 states by 73 interviewers
10. An analysis derived from the summary tabulations of the completed interview forms (see p. 27-53, "Interviews")

10

11. An analysis of the team evaluations (see p. 54-71, "Team Evaluations")
12. Seven group discussions for team members (in New York, Atlanta, Chicago, and San Francisco) with an analysis and interpretation of their reactions (see "Group Discussions, " p. 71-88, and Appendix E)
13. Review of all data and preparation of the final Phase I report by the staff, consultants, and principal advisors to the project.

All agencies known to have in operation, to be planning, or even to have closed facilities with at least one relevant feature of a center were identified from the following sources:

ESEA Titles I, II, and III Project Reports filed with the USOE
Public libraries serving a population of 30, 000 or more
State and provincial public library agencies
College and university schools of library science
State school library supervisors
State coordinators of audiovisual programs
State superintendents of public instruction
Superintendents of operating local public school systems with 10, 000 pupils or more
Publishers' mailing lists of review copies of childrens' and young adult trade books
Recommendations from the American Association of School Librarians (American Library Association), the Department of Audiovisual Instruction (National Education Association), and from individuals associated with schools of library science, and with state library, audiovisual, and educational agencies
Individual requests by educational agencies.

A sample first questionnaire was developed by the project staff with assistance from consultants and the Executive Advisory Council. The principal purpose of this questionnaire was to identify, from among the sources cited earlier, those agencies which gave evidence of one or more components of a media selection center. The sample questionnaire was tested in Florida and Pennsylvania, states in which the investigators knew media selection center activities were being carried on. State school library supervisors in these states cooperated in the initial identification and follow-up processes. Initial mailings for the sample study totaled 226 and final returns totaled 166, or 74 percent.

The revised first questionnaire then was mailed to the 1,995 agencies identified as possible media selection centers (but excluding those in Florida and Pennsylvania). The total returned (after two follow-up mailings) was 1,583; the overall return (including pretest) was 79 percent. The returned questionnaires were analyzed to determine the agency which demonstrated one or more viable components of a media selection center as defined in this project. In this way, 1,145 respondents were eliminated. Principal criteria for elimination were:

Agency disqualified itself
Agency provided no staffing for center
Center was strictly a materials dissemination outlet with no selection services or programs for any instructional medium
Agency was financially unsupported, operating on donations only
Two or more agencies with differing addresses were found to be operating a single center, in which instances the duplicating citations were eliminated.

An analysis was made from a summary tabulation of the data from the 484 agencies which displayed one or more components of a media selection center (see p. 19-22, "Mail Questionnaire Surveys - First Questionnaire").

A sample second questionnaire was developed by the project staff with assistance from consultants and the Executive Advisory Council. The principal purpose of this questionnaire was to define a more precise profile of the quantitative aspects of each agency studied with particular reference to instructional media and equipment holdings, personnel, physical plant or facilities, funding, and use made of services. A secondary purpose was to collect data which would serve as the basis for identifying those agencies which would serve as appropriate subjects for on-site qualitative examination. This second questionnaire was tested in Florida and Pennsylvania in a small sample of agencies known to have one or more strong media selection center components. In each instance, more than one respondent per agency was requested to complete the questionnaire, and the resulting responses were compared for inconsistencies in interpretation and response.

The sample questionnaire was revised and a second sample was undertaken of the 46 agencies not eliminated in the analysis of Florida and Pennsylvania responses to the first questionnaire. As a result of an analysis of this test sample response, a third and final revision of the second questionnaire was made.

The revised second questionnaire was mailed to the 440 remaining agencies not eliminated in the analysis of the first questionnaire. Recipients of the second questionnaire included public school systems, district and regional public libraries, state departments of education, and teacher education institutions. One general follow-up mailing and approximately 50 follow-up telephone calls were made. The total number of questionnaires returned was 354 (as of 1 December 1969), an overall return of 79 percent.

Analysis of the returned questionnaires was made to determine the extent of quantitative data reflected by the centers' responses in the areas of collections (regardless of media mix), audiovisual equipment, personnel, physical plant facilities, funding, and free materials and equipment. Those agencies reporting quantitative data which did not reflect one or more significant activities of a media selection center (with particular regard to collections, personnel, and use) were eliminated. An additional number eliminated themselves as not applicable. Total deleted: 142. An analysis was made from a summary tabulation of the 212 remaining centers (see "Mail Questionnaire Surveys - Second Questionnaire," p. 23-25).

Two- and three-man survey teams selected by the project director and project coordinator, with recommendations made by the Executive Advisory Council, visited 38 different centers which showed promise of successful components of an EMSC program. The list of centers visited is as follows:

1. Phoenix Indian School, Phoenix, Ariz.
2. Instructional Aids Department, San Diego City Schools, San Diego, Calif.
3. Audio-Visual Services and School Library Service, San Diego County Department of Education, San Diego, Calif.
4. Sonoma County Instructional Materials Center, Santa Rosa, Calif.
5. Educational Development Center, Daytona Beach, Fla.

13

6. University of Florida Educational Media Center, Gainesville, Fla.
7. Alachua County Instructional Media Center, Gainesville, Fla.
8. Instructional Media Center, Jacksonville, Fla.
9. Educational Media Center, Hillsborough County Schools, Tampa, Fla.
10. Educational Media Center, Sarasota County Schools, Sarasota, Fla.
11. Materials Center, Broward County Schools, Fort Lauderdale, Fla.
12. Fulton County Educational Media Center, Fulton County Schools, Atlanta, Ga.
13. Alton Area Supplementary Center, Alton, Ill.
14. Instructional Media Center, East St. Louis, Ill.
15. Wabash Valley Educational Center, West Lafayette, Ind.
16. Southwest Iowa Learning Center, Red Oak, Iowa
17. Library Service, Waterloo Community School District, Waterloo, Iowa
18. Book Examination Center, State Department of Education, Topeka, Kans.
19. Examination Center, State Department of Education, Baton Rouge, La.
20. Bossier Parish Educational Resources Center, Bossier City, La.
21. Flint Public Library, Flint, Mich.
22. Book Evaluation Center, Lansing, Mich.
23. Materials Selection Center, Omaha Public Schools, Omaha, Nebr.
24. Instructional Material Preview Center, Rochester, N.Y.
25. BOCES #1, Yorktown Heights, N.Y.
26. Center for Learning Resources, State Department of Public Instruction, Raleigh, N.C.
27. Cuyahoga County Public Library, Cleveland, Ohio
28. Curriculum Media Center, Oklahoma City Public Schools, Okla.
29. Central Area Branch Examination Center, Division of School Libraries, State Department of Public Instruction, Harrisburg, Pa.
30. Pedagogical Library, City District Board of Education, Philadelphia, Pa.
31. Western Area Branch, Division of School Libraries, State Department of Public Instruction, Pittsburgh, Pa.

14

32. Intermountain Indian School, Bureau of Indian Affairs, Brigham City, Utah
33. Bureau of Teaching Materials, State Department of Education, Richmond, Va.
34. Highline School District Research Center, Seattle, Wash.
35. Instructional Materials Center, Monongalia County Schools, Morgantown, W. Va.
36. Cooperative Children's Book Center, Madison, Wis.
37. University of Wisconsin Instructional Media Laboratory, Milwaukee, Wis.
38. Instructional Materials Center, Racine Public School System, Racine, Wis.

Subsequently, 12 additional places received team visits:

1. Instructional Aids Library, Los Angeles City Schools, Los Angeles, Calif. (2 visits)
2. School Libraries and Instructional Materials, Hawaii State Department of Education, Honolulu, Hawaii
3. Instructional Materials Center, Vigo County School Corporation, Terre Haute, Ind.
4. Area VIII Instructional Materials Center, Dubuque, Iowa
5. Department of Educational Media, Montgomery County Public Schools, Rockville, Md.
6. Instructional Media Center, Educational Service Unit No. 2, Freemont, Nebr.
7. Educational Development Center, Paramus Public Schools, Paramus, N. J.
8. Bank Street Multi-Media Materials Center, New York, N. Y.
9. University of North Carolina Media Center at Greensboro, Greensboro, N. C.
10. Eastern Area Branch, Division of School Libraries, State Department of Public Instruction, Upper Darby, Pa. (2 visits)
11. Educational and Cultural Center, Pittsylvania School District, Chatham, Va.
12. Instructional Materials Center, Madison Public Schools, Madison, Wis.

(The number of centers unwilling or unable to receive a team visit was negligible.) Each survey team included a librarian

15

or a media specialist and a teacher, curriculum specialist, or school administrator, one of whom was designated as chairman. Sites were selected to reflect a geographical, administrative, and program variety. Though three surveyors were originally assigned to each visit, table 1 shows the actual number of team members per center visit.

TABLE 1
On-site Visits

Number of centers visited	38
Number of team members	73
Number of centers visited by 2 team members	11
Number of centers visited by 3 team members	27

Two interview questionnaires were provided, one for interviewing the center director and the center staff, the other for interviewing the users - the curriculum specialist, classroom teacher, media specialist/librarian, administrator, school principal (see Appendix C for these). A group evaluation form was also provided for the team's joint evaluation (see Appendix D).

The project staff had intended to conduct a series of advance briefings for the survey teams, but was unable to schedule them. Some team members subsequently recommended that everyone be briefed on interviewing techniques including the use of a questionnaire.

The analysis in table 2 is based upon interviews conducted by the various visiting team members with two categories of respondents - the "in group," consisting of center directors and staff in the 38 centers visited, and the "out group," the users of the center and administrators. [3] The 91 "in group" interviews is a total of 38 center directors and 53 center staff members.

In addition, 212 interviews were conducted with various "users" and school administrators. The occupational classification of the "user" or "out group" included interviews with 20 school administrators, 46 principals, 59 media specialists/librarians, 45 teachers, and 42 curriculum specialists.

_____

3. The terms "in group" and "out group" are commonly used in opinion research and have no pejorative connotation in this report.

16

The prime purpose of the interview was to obtain information about the center, its services, and its users. The "in group" questionnaire consisted of 39 questions (see p. 125-36, Appendix C). The "out group" questionnaire consisted of 29 questions which were either identical or derivative (see p. 137-61, Appendix C). The purpose in using two questionnaires as similar as possible was to establish by comparison the extent of knowledge existing in both groups.

Accordingly, the data report the results for the total of 303 respondents interviewed including the 91 "in group" and 212 "out group" respondents (table 2).

TABLE 2
Interviews Conducted

Total "In Group"	91
Center directors interviewed	38
Center staff interviewed	53
Total "Out Group"	212
Administrators	20
Principals	46
Media specialists/librarians	59
Teachers	45
Curriculum specialists	42
Total number of interviews conducted	303

In addition, the group evaluation form (see Appendix D) allowed for an arbitrary scoring system that conceivably might separate the better centers from the poorer ones. The top third of the centers that received higher ratings (approaching excellent on the scale) were then compared with the lower third of the centers, those approaching poor on the scale (see p. 27-54, "Interviews"). It is to be noted that the data reported in the tables are based upon responses rather than respondents. For some questions, multiple responses were reported; for other questions, multiple responses were not reported.

All site surveyors were invited to participate in seven group discussions (content analysis sessions) which were held in New York, Chicago, Atlanta, and San Francisco. Of the 38 centers visited, 36 centers were represented by the 49 group discussion participants.

17

A panel leader's guide (see Appendix E) was prepared to elicit the reactions and attitudes of the 49 group discussion participants with respect to the value of the interview forms, the interviewers' responses, shared experiences, and comparisons of the centers visited. The group discussions were recorded on tape and analyzed for recurring themes. Table 3 shows the number of centers visited by each team member participating in the group discussion.

TABLE 3
Number of Centers Visited by Team Members

Team members visiting one center	26
Team members visiting two centers	16
Team members visiting three centers	5
Team members visiting four centers	0
Team members visiting five centers	2
Total	49

All quantitative and qualitative procedures (used to achieve a combined methodology that was additive rather than discrete) were reported to and reviewed by the Executive Advisory Council at three meetings, the first in Kansas City in June 1968, immediately following approval of the project by USOE; the others in New York City in September 1968, and August 1969. The formal Advisory Committee has met twice - 2 October 1969 and 25-26 January 1970.

Public information activities included distribution of 25,000 copies of an explanatory brochure (Appendix F), a briefing for the education press in September 1968, and periodic press releases.

2
Findings
and
Analyses

MAIL QUESTIONNAIRE SURVEYS

First Questionnaire

Since the objective of Phase I was to obtain information about the nature and characteristics of educational media selection centers, the responses from a sampling of 484 questionnaires were analyzed. Analysis revealed that such centers were located in all the geographic regions of the United States, as presented in table 4. The data indicate media centers are more numerous in the south Atlantic, the east north-central, the Pacific, and the middle Atlantic states. They are less numerous in the east south-central and mountain states.

TABLE 4
Regional Location of 484 Centers

	Percentage of Centers
East north-central	17
South Atlantic	17
Pacific	15
Middle Atlantic	14
West south-central	10
West north-central	9
New England	7
Mountain	6
East south-central	5

Among the 484 centers, the most frequent affiliation is with a public school system. Table 5 indicates the nature of

19

the administrative unit in which the centers function, that is, the kind of educational organization with which they are affiliated.

The 484 media centers most frequently serve a local area or a county area. Table 6 presents the geographic areas served by the various centers.

TABLE 5
Media Center Affiliations

	Percentage of Centers
Public school	58
Public library	12
College and university	11
State dept. of education	9
County school district	4
Other	6

TABLE 6
Geographic Areas Served

	Percentage of Centers
Local	38
County	24
Regional	18
State	16
National	2
No response	2

Almost two-thirds of the 484 centers maintain collections that are intended for elementary and secondary schools. Adding post-secondary school levels accounts for almost nine of every ten centers (table 7).

TABLE 7
Level of Material in Collection

	Percentage of Centers
Elementary & secondary combined	63
All 3 levels	23
Elementary only	7
Secondary only	3
Postsecondary only	2
No response	2

More than half of the 484 centers employ from one to three full-time persons and one or two part-time employees. Table 8 presents the distribution of full- and part-time personnel employed by the centers.

A considerable variation exists in the funding sources for the operation of various centers. More than half of the 484 centers are funded by a combination of sources; the rest have a single source of funds - most often a local agency. A center funded by more than one source generally results from federal monies added to either state or local support. Table 9 presents the source or sources of funding for responding centers.

TABLE 8
Full and Part-time Employees of Centers

Number of Employees	Percentage of Centers	
	Full-time Employees	Part-time Employees
0	20	60
1	26	17
2	18	9
3	12	5
4	6	2
5	4	2
6-10	11	3
Over 10	3	2

TABLE 9
Sources of Funding

	Percentage of Centers
Sole source	
Local	19
Federal	10
State	8
Private	3
	40
Combination of sources	
Federal, local, & state	16
Federal & local	13
Local & state	8
Federal & state	8
Private & federal	2
Private, federal, local, & state	2
Private & local	1
Private, local, & state	1
Private, federal, & local	1
None	8
Total	100

The hours of operation for the majority of the 484 centers extend beyond the usual school hours. Table 10 indicates that 70 percent of the centers operate during and after school hours.

TABLE 10
Center Hours of Operation

	Percentage of Centers
School hours & after hours	70
During school hours only	24
No answer	6

A checklist of six types of materials available for use was asked for in the questionnaire. The most frequent types of materials identified were print materials, excluding textbooks, and professional and/or curriculum materials. Table 11 presents the materials available in the 484 centers.

TABLE 11
Materials Available in Centers

	Percentage of Centers
Print materials	
Print materials, excluding textbooks	88
Professional or curriculum media	81
Textbooks	59
Programmed instruction	51
Nonprint materials	
16mm films	63
Other audiovisual media	77

The most frequent source of in-service training is that which is scheduled on request (41 percent). Regularly scheduled in-service training occurs 15 percent of the time. It appears from the responses that probably 85 percent of the 484 centers have some form of in-service training. The center staffs also serve in a consultant capacity, either at the center or in the field.

Second Questionnaire

The second questionnaire was mailed to 440 centers and returned by 354 centers. Each respondent was asked to furnish estimates with reference to inventories of various types of media. The questionnaire returns indicated a wide variation within each of the media categories so it was decided to merely report the modal frequency of those reporting any of that type of media as a guide for future inquiry and analysis. Table 12 presents, for each of the media types, the modal (i.e., most frequent) frequency as well as the percentages of the centers within that modal frequency.

TABLE 12

Center Ownership of Specific Media Type

Media Owned	Modal Frequency	Percentage of Centers
Hardbound books other than textbooks	under 2000	29
Paperback books of any type	under 300	42
Textbooks (except programmed texts)	1000-4999	20
Professional books	under 300	25
Professional books	1000-4999	25
Curriculum guides	400-799	26
Periodicals	100-299	26
Programmed instruction	under 50	29
Other printed instructional media	under 100	13
Photographs, pictorial, or graphic works	under 100	14
Art prints	under 50	15
Study prints	under 50	18
Maps	under 25	23
Charts	under 25	21
Globes	under 10	30
Filmstrips	1000-4999	25
Slides	1000+	18
Slides	under 100	18
Disc recordings	under 100	23
Tape recordings	under 100	30
Transparencies	under 300	30
16mm films	1000-4999	28
8mm films	50-199	25
Kinescopes	under 10	6
Video tapes	under 10	10
Microfilm	under 100	10
Realia	under 25	16
Reference books	under 50	24

Table 13 similarly presents the modal frequencies and percentages of centers reporting ownership within each category of audiovisual equipment.

TABLE 13
Center Ownership of Specific Audiovisual Equipment

Equipment	Modal Frequency	Percentage of Centers
Filmstrip projectors	under 5	38
Slide projectors	under 5	48
Filmstrip viewers	under 5	46
Film projectors - 16mm	under 5	44
Film projectors - 8mm	under 5	52
Disc record players	under 5	43
Tape recorders and players	under 5	35
Television receivers	under 5	36
Videotape recorders	under 5	39
Overhead projectors	under 5	40
Opaque projectors	under 5	45
Microreader	under 5	40
Microreader-printer	under 5	28

The questionnaire also sought to obtain leads with reference to existing facilities and the approximate square footage of such facilities. Table 14 presents the findings and will allow for further and more accurate investigation in incorporating these space requirements into the "Guide" (Phase II), now in preparation.

TABLE 14
Estimated Modal Square Footage of Facilities

	Percentage of Center Housing Such Facility	Modal Square Footage Reported
Open shelving area(s)	89	200-699
Reading room(s)	65	500-999
Group viewing & listening area(s)	76	100-299
Individual viewing & listening area(s)	57	under 100
Materials production area(s)	66	1000+
In-service training classroom(s)	55	500-1999
Materials processing area(s)	78	200-699

Teachers make heaviest use of the center collections, but

all three groups (teachers, librarians, and other adults) use the services nearly equally (table 15).

TABLE 15
Estimated Use of Collection and Services

	Percentage of User Group		
	Librarians	Teachers	Other Adults
Use of Collection			
Heavy	32	53	27
Moderate	48	32	49
Light	10	8	14
No answer	10	7	10
Use of Services			
Heavy	40	39	35
Moderate	38	36	40
Light	9	13	12
No answer	13	12	13

It is clear that a media center requires both print and audio-visual media and in equal proportions as indicated in table 16.

TABLE 16
Types of Materials Most in Demand

	Percentage of Centers
Print	32
Audiovisual	33
Both	24
No answer	11

Based upon the four points investigated it would appear that the respondent centers offer individual advice, workshops, and evaluation of current media in about eight out of ten instances (table 17).

TABLE 17
Services Offered by Centers

	Percentage of Centers
Advice to individual	85
Workshops	79
Evaluation of current media	78
Retrospective evaluation of media	56

RATIONALE FOR ON-SITE INTERVIEWS

Up to this point the study has involved only quantitative data gathered to identify centers and to determine in some detail the kinds of materials, number of personnel, and other information relating to the function of media selection and evaluation in these centers. However, if adequate evidence was to be found for the development of a guide to be used to develop or improve media selection centers (the objective of Phase II), it was essential to take a closer look at a small sample of centers by means of on-site observation and analysis.

To accomplish this, the director selected 38 centers from those responding to the second questionnaire, for on-site visits by survey teams. Selection of the 38 centers was not on a random basis, but rather on the basis of specific criteria: (1) willingness to be visited (this question was asked in the second questionnaire); (2) evidence in the second questionnaire that a center possessed one or more components for potential effectiveness of success; (3) representation of geographic areas and types of agencies; (4) assurance of inclusion of certain special categories, such as Indian schools, public libraries, special education centers, and the like; (5) inclusion of different levels of development or possibilities of useful comparison or contrast.

The purpose of the on-site visits was to confirm, correct, or expand the data (especially on program of services) given in the second questionnaire, to determine the attitudes and opinions of the staff and the users of centers, and to provide cross-reference of the quantitative findings wherever possible. It was anticipated that only by on-site visits could the necessary

26

depth of insight and interpretation be gained for development
of the projected "Guide" (Phase II).

Tne findings of the on-site visits are reported in the following three sections:

Interviews - a report of the data gathered during interviews
with center directors and staff and different kinds of
adult users (see p. 27-54)
Team Evaluations - a summary of the team evaluations of
each center (see p. 54-71)
Group Discussions - a further analysis of the experiences
of the on-site survey teams secured by face-to-face
group discussion (see p. 71-88).

INTERVIEWS

The analyses which follow are based upon interviews conducted by the various visiting team members with two categories
of respondents - the "in group"and the "out group." The "in
group" consisted of center directors and their staffs in the 38
centers visited. The 91 individuals in this category included
38 center directors and 53 center staff members.

In addition, 212 interviews were conducted with various
users of centers or administrators who were responsible for
the activities and funding of centers. The occupational classification of the user or "out group"included 20 administrators,
46 principals, 59 media specialists/librarians, 45 teachers,
and 42 curriculum specialists.

The prime purpose of the interview was to obtain information about the center, its services, and its users. The "in
group" questionnaire consisted of 39 questions (see p. 125-36,
Appendix C). The "out group"form consisted of 29 questions
that were either identical to those asked of center personnel
or derivative of them (see p. 137-61, Appendix C).

Two such similar questionnaires were used to establish by
comparison the extent of knowledge existing in both the "in"
and "out groups." Accordingly, the data is presented by reporting the results for the total of 303 respondents interviewed as
well as the 91 "in group" and 212 "out group"respondents.

In addition, the team evaluation form (see Appendix D)
allowed for an arbitrary scoring system which conceivably

27

might separate the better centers from the poorer centers. The top third of the centers that received higher ratings (approaching excellent on the scale) were then compared with the lower third of the centers (those approaching poor on the scale).

It is to be noted that the data reported in the tables are percentages based upon responses rather than respondents. For all questions where multiple responses were possible, multiple responses were reported. For example, the answer to the question "Who are the frequent users of this center?" can be expected to include more than one occupational group - teachers, media specialists, curriculum specialists, school administrators, and other professionals.

Tables 18-49, which follow, present highlights of the findings resulting from the on-site interviews conducted by the visiting teams. The paragraph or two of text that usually precedes the individual table summarizes the major finding of that table.

Major Findings Based on Interviews

The most frequent users of centers are teachers (45%). Administrators and supervisors (21%) and librarians/audio-visual specialists (18%) are the second most frequent categories of users. The "out group" tends to indicate that teachers use the center somewhat more than the "in group" indicates (47% to 40%). The centers rated in the top third and those rated in the lower third are not differentiable according to usage by category. This could mean either that all centers serve a useful function or that users have no choice in selecting a better center in preference to a poorer center (table 18).

The two major reasons for using a center are (1) for evaluation and review of media available (24%) and (2) for media resources not available elsewhere (20%). The "out group" tends to state these two items as reasons somewhat more often than does center staff. No meaningful pattern of differentiation exists among the high and low rated centers (table 19).

An increase in competency of the users is attributed to being better informed about media (25%) and as an aid in establishing criteria for selection (20%). The "out group" tends to indicate these reasons more frequently than the "in group" attributes these reasons to the "out group."

28

TABLE 18
Frequent Users of Centers

(Number of Responses)	Percentage of Responses			Team Rating of Center	
	Total (569)	"In Group" (190)	"Out Group" (379)	Percent in Top Third (229)	Percent in Lower Third (177)
Teachers	45	40	47	45	42
Administrative staff and supervisors	21	22	21	21	19
Librarians/audiovisual specialists	18	17	19	16	21
College classes	5	8	4	7	6
Student teachers	5	5	4	5	6
Center staff	3	4	3	4	3
State Department of Education staff	2	3	1	1	2
All others	1	1	1	1	1

TABLE 19
Reasons for Using Centers

(Number of Responses)	Percentage of Responses			Team Rating of Center	
	Total (519)	"In Group" (141)	"Out Group" (378)	Percent in Top Third (202)	Percent in Lower Third (166)
Evaluation, review of media available	24	19	25	19	25
Media available in centers not found in individual schools	20	16	22	22	20
Concentration of media in one location	14	13	14	15	14
To improve teaching materials	11	11	11	12	11
In-service training in media & equipment	9	11	8	8	9
Provides profession materials for planning self-improvement	8	12	7	9	6
Borrow to test classroom value	7	8	6	7	6
Convenience	4	6	4	4	7
Research	3	4	3	4	2

On the other hand, increases in teaching competency are more often indicated by the "in group" than by the "out group" themselves. This may be a critical issue and one must question whether increasing competency of selection and evaluation is the same thing as increasing teaching effectiveness. It probably is not.

It is also to be noted that more of the "out group" than the "in group" tend not to answer this question, the inference being that users may question that the center increases their competency. A comparison of higher and lower rated centers indicates that the top third centers more frequently state "professional materials have stimulated teaching methods" (21% to 11%) and the lower third centers more often indicate a "no answer" (21% to 8%) (table 20).

TABLE 20
Effect of Center on User Competency

(Number of Responses)	Percentage of Responses			Team Rating of Center	
	Total (303)	"In Group" (89)	"Out Group" (214)	Percent in Top Third (116)	Percent in Lower Third (100)
Became better informed about media	25	18	28	24	29
Helped establish criteria for selection	20	14	23	19	20
Professional materials have stimulated teaching methods	15	21	13	21	11
Integration of media into class instruction	10	17	8	10	8
Selection policy allows better use of school collection	7	13	3	7	3
Teaching assisted by curriculum guides provided	4	6	3	4	3
Increased knowledge of teaching/learning process	2	2	2	3	2
More and better media available due to center's funding	2	4	1	3	1
Confident of selection policy	2	2	2	1	2
No answer	13	3	17	8	21

About 70 percent of the centers indicate that more than 300 persons visit a center during a typical month (table 21).

TABLE 21
Frequency of Center's Usage

| | Percentage of Responses | Team Rating of Center | |
| | "In Group" | Percent in Top Third | Percent in Lower Third |
(Number of Responses)	(65)	(28)	(15)
80 or fewer	3	3	-
81-150	12	11	7
151-200	6	4	20
201-300	8	11	-
301 and more	71	71	73

About half of the 38 centers are open during the day, whereas the remainder have additional hours, most usually by appointment. The top rated centers more often arrange for additional hours than do the centers rated in the lower third (table 22).

TABLE 22
Hours Center is Open

| | Percentage of Responses | Team Rating of Center | |
| | "In Group" | Percent in Top Third | Percent in Lower Third |
(Number of Responses)	(85)	(33)	(24)
Full day	47	37	58
Full day, plus by appointment	24	36	17
Full day, plus evenings	4	3	4
Full day, plus weekends	3	3	4
Full day, plus evenings and weekends	1	-	-
Full day, plus other combination of hours	21	21	17

The "in group" tends to allocate its time to administration quite differently. One-fifth indicates it spends about 20 percent on administration, and, at the other extreme, one-fifth spends about 100 percent on administration. The lower third of the centers have more of the "in group" spending 21 percent to 30 percent of their time on administration, whereas the top third more often spends 61 percent to 70 percent on administration.

However, in the 20 percent or less or 80 percent or more time spent on administration, very little difference between the top and lower third of the centers is found (table 23).

TABLE 23
Percentage of Time Spent on Administration

| (Number of Responses) | Percentage of Responses | Team Rating of Center | |
	"In Group" (89)	Percent in Top Third (35)	Percent in Lower Third (25)
0-10%	15	0	13
11-20	7	14	4
21-30	13	6	29
31-40	7	6	8
41-60	8	11	8
61-70	11	20	–
71-80	15	17	13
81-90	4	3	4
91-100	20	23	21

Apparently, as table 24 indicates, spending more time with users is important since the centers rated in the top third much

TABLE 24
Percentage of Time Spent with Users

| (Number of Responses) | Percentage of Responses | Team Rating of Center | |
	"In Group" (68)	Percent in Top Third (28)	Percent in Lower Third (18)
0-10%	16	14	23
11-20	18	21	12
21-30	21	21	23
31-40	16	10	23
41-60	12	17	6
61-70	9	10	6
71-80	1	4	–
81-90	6	–	–
91-100	1	–	6

more often spend their time (41% to 90%) with users compared to the centers rated in the lower third (11% to 30%).

To gain an idea of the specific activities considered as major on any one day, the respondents were asked, "Talking about yesterday, what was your major activity?" A long list of activities resulted. This is reproduced to present the variety of ways in which time is occupied on any one day.

Preparing budget for new programs
Preparing educational television services
Answering telephone queries
Preparing talk and presentation on education
Arranging to have center operating if threatened teacher strike occurs
At state meeting for educational supervisors
Drawing up and discussing policy statements
Planning series of in-service workshops
Cataloging
Conferences
Reviewed materials for center collection
Consulted with planners for new schools
At regional curriculum meeting
Met with sales representatives
Planning insurance program
Paper work
Reviewing new computer printout of catalog
Reference service
Working on delivery problems, scheduling
Planning information exchange data bank
Supervisory, administrative duties
Reviewing payroll
Arranging new catalog format
Staff meeting
Meeting with new teachers
Planning new special programs
Planning librarians meeting
Worked with committee to develop state-wide services
Planning internship program
Worked with evaluation committee
Preparing orders for materials
Student visited a school to view materials
Conference with Lindery representative
Consult with reviewers of films being considered

Demonstrated audiovisual equipment
Materials production
Sent audiovisual directory out to schools
Book mending
Writing report for state education department
In-service training classes or workshop
Constructing audiovisual maintenance program
Processing materials
Physical housekeeping tasks
Consulted with principals and teachers
Putting on television courses
Planning for addition to building
Assigned materials to schools.

The "in group" reports that a written job specification exists in about two-thirds of the centers; few differences occur between the top and lower third centers in this respect (table 25).

TABLE 25
Existence of Written Job Specification

	Percentage of Responses	Team Rating of Center	
	"In Group"	Percent in Top Third	Percent in Lower Third
(Number of Responses)	(86)	(34)	(25)
Yes	70	65	68
No	30	35	32

Coordination/planning of programs and administration of services account for 45 percent of the major responsibilities of the "in group." These activities are similar for the centers rated in the top third and in the lower third. However, as indicated in table 26, differences occur since supervisory duties more often occupy the top center staffs (23% to 10%) and those in the lower third centers more often assist and instruct by telephone (12% to 4%), or serve as consultant to users in the field (23% to 11%).

34

TABLE 26
Major Job Responsibilities

(Number of Responses)	Percentage of Responses "In Group" (133)	Team Rating of Center Percent in Top Third (53)	Percent in Lower Third (40)
Coordination, planning of programs	23	23	18
Administration of services	22	21	23
Supervisory duties	17	23	10
Consultant to users in field	16	11	23
Media reviewing, selection	10	11	8
Assisting, instructing users at center, by phone	6	4	12
Purchase of media	4	5	2
Liaison between center staff and administration	1	2	2
Materials design	1	-	2

The top and lower third of the centers tend to have equivalent percentages when categories of staff with M.A. and M.A. plus degrees are combined. More center staff in the top third of the centers fall in the M.A. plus category (table 27).

TABLE 27
Staff Degrees or Professional Training

(Number of Responses)	Percentage of Responses Total (291)	"In Group" (86)	"Out Group" (205)	Team Rating of Center Percent in Top Third (115)	Percent in Lower Third (98)
M.A.	62	52	67	57	68
M.A. plus	14	27	9	18	8
B.A.	11	11	11	12	11
B.A. postgraduate courses	7	6	8	9	5
Ph.D.	5	3	5	4	8
Less than B.A.	1	1	-	-	-

The center staffs indicate that library experience (20%), knowledge of curriculum planning (20%), along with audiovisual and media training (17%) and business administration or personnel training (16%), are the four kinds of additional professional training that would be most beneficial.

The staffs at the centers rated in the top third are more desirous of knowledge of curriculum planning; whereas the staffs at the centers rated in the lower third want more library experience and audiovisual retraining (table 28).

TABLE 28
Beneficial Additional Education

(Number of Responses)	Percentage of Responses	Team Rating of Center	
	"In Group" (115)	Percent in Top Third (47)	Percent in Lower Third (32)
Library experience	20	11	25
Knowledge of curriculum planning	20	26	9
Audiovisual and other media training	17	19	22
Business administration, personnel management	16	19	13
Automation, mechanization	12	15	12
Audiovisual and other media retraining	10	4	16
Children and young adult literature courses	3	4	3
Photography, graphic arts	2	2	-

The "in group" tends to place greater emphasis on "make teachers aware of wide variety of media to enrich teaching" as a major goal than does the "out group" (38% to 26%). There do not seem to be any clear-cut differences between the centers rated in the top and lower third with respect to major goals (table 29).

36

TABLE 29
Major Goals of Center

(Number of Responses)	Percentage of Responses			Team Rating of Center	
	Total (484)	"In Group" (128)	"Out Group" (356)	Percent in Top Third (191)	Percent in Lower Third (152)
Make teachers aware of wide variety of media to enrich teaching	29	38	26	29	27
Make samples available for review, evaluation	14	9	16	12	17
Provide information for proposed curriculum changes	10	9	11	11	9
Support work of curriculum consultants	9	12	8	12	7
Distribute media to schools	8	6	9	5	9
Training in use of media	7	5	7	6	9
Media available for classroom use	6	5	7	7	6
Provide, stimulate professional leadership among users	6	4	7	8	5
Centralized processing services provided	3	2	3	2	3
Provide resources for advanced training, research	3	5	2	3	3
Answer requests of users	3	3	2	2	3
Philosophical or attitudinal changes	2	2	2	3	2

It appears, as table 30 indicates, that the centers are involved in five major activities - distribution of media, evaluation, consulting, training, and exhibiting materials. No
differences are found between the "in group" and "out group"
in their statements of the centers' major activities. Further,
no appreciable differences are found between the centers
rated in the top third and in the lower third with the possible
exception that those in the lower third more often assist in reviewing and evaluating media (25% to 17%).

TABLE 30
Major Activities of Center

	Percentage of Responses			Team Rating of Center	
		"In	"Out	Percent in	Percent in
	Total	Group"	Group"	Top Third	Lower Third
(Number of Responses)	(613)	(196)	(417)	(247)	(188)
Circulate, distribute media	21	20	21	19	16
Review and evaluate media	19	18	20	17	25
Consultant to schools	16	14	17	18	15
Training in use of media	15	13	15	16	14
Provide exhibits, displays of materials	13	11	14	13	13
Materials design, production	8	12	6	8	6
Acquainting student teachers with media	4	6	4	6	5
Obtain items requested by users	2	3	2	2	4
Maintain equipment	2	3	1	1	2

The one service offering the center's greatest contribution
is considered to be the distribution of media. However, the
"in group" and "out group" are in disagreement. The "out
group" ranks such distribution first with 28 percent whereas
the "in group" ranks this fourth with 16 percent. The "in
group" gives higher ranking to "reviews, evaluation, criteria
for selection," "keeping teachers informed," and "training in
the use of media."

A comparison of the centers in the top third and the lower
third shows that the top rated centers rank training higher
than do those rated in the lower third (17% to 10%). Conversely,

the centers rated in the lower third rank media distribution and evaluation higher (table 31).

TABLE 31
The Service Contributing Most to the Center's Educational Program

(Number of Responses)	Percentage of Responses			Team Rating of Center	
	Total (273)	"In Group" (79)	"Out Group" (194)	Percent in Top Third (106)	Percent in Lower Third (89)
Circulate, distribute media	25	16	28	18	23
Review and evaluation criteria for selection	16	20	14	15	24
Keeping teachers informed	15	19	14	17	15
Exposure via displays	14	8	16	12	13
Training in use of media	13	23	9	17	10
Availability of material to support curriculum	8	6	9	11	6
Selection process to acquaint users with good media	5	4	5	4	6
Obtain items requested	2	3	3	3	3
Materials design	2	1	2	3	1

The specific services to be offered in the coming year primarily are continuations of existing programs (26%). However, as table 32 indicates, the "in group" more often refers to

TABLE 32
Specific Service Offered

(Number of Responses)	Percentage of Responses			Team Rating of Center	
	Total (288)	"In Group" (89)	"Out Group" (199)	Percent in Top Third (114)	Percent in Lower Third (93)
Continue current programs	26	16	31	25	24
Special workshops to introduce media	18	22	16	21	14
Distribution of lists of evaluated media	9	14	7	6	14
Training users through workshops, classes, etc.	8	13	5	12	4
New media introduced in a specific subject	7	5	8	9	5
Media production	6	8	5	4	4
Delivery service to schools	5	8	3	3	7
More and improved publicity, information services	4	5	3	4	5
No answer	17	9	21	16	23

39

special workshops (22%) while the "out group" most frequently refers to program continuation (31%) or does not answer (21%). A comparison of the top third and lower third centers indicates that the top third more often plans special workshops (21% to 14%), while the lower third more often plans distribution of lists of evaluated materials (14% to 6%).

The major new service being planned is "increased evaluation of media and programs" (33%). The next three add up to another 36 percent - new exhibits, cooperative programs with colleges, and closed circuit television. The new services differentiating the centers rated in the top third and those rated in the lower third are cooperative programs with colleges which are planned more often by the top third centers (18% to 0%), and "expand use of computer" and "produce catalog, " which are planned more often by the lower third (table 33).

TABLE 33
New Services Planned within Coming Year

(Number of Responses)	Percentage of Responses "In Group" (73)	Team Rating of Center	
		Percent in Top Third (28)	Percent in Lower Third (21)
Increased evaluation of media and programs	33	39	38
New displays, exhibits	14	11	10
Cooperative program with colleges	12	18	-
Closed circuit television	10	4	10
Expand use of computer	5	4	14
Subject assistance offered to user in selection processes	5	-	5
Initiate new reading education program	6	11	5
Produce catalog of holdings	6	4	14
Increase, improve in-service training	4	3	4
Extend availability by regions in mobile components	4	3	-
No answer	1	3	-

About 50 percent of the respondents indicate that their role in the decisions to offer new services is "to make recommendations to the supervisor" (table 34).

TABLE 34
Role in the Decision to Offer New Services

	Percentage of Responses			Team Rating of Center	
(Number of Responses)	Total (252)	"In Group" (81)	"Out Group" (171)	Percent in Top Third (101)	Percent in Lower Third (82)
Make recommendations to supervisor	53	51	54	52	49
Advisor or consultant to user, staff	24	11	30	24	29
Design, develop new programs	11	21	6	13	9
Accept, reject proposals from staff, users	5	7	4	5	5
Coordinate planning for new programs	5	6	4	5	6
Assign money, personnel to carry out plans	2	4	2	1	2

The "out group" tends to be unfamiliar with services that were offered and discarded (table 35). For example, 36 percent of the "in group" responses in contrast to 71 percent of the "out group" responses indicate that no services have been discarded, and 36 percent of the "in group" responses in contrast to 14 percent of the "out group" responses indicate that lending filmstrips has been discontinued since schools have their own.

The centers rated in the lower third tend not to have discarded services slightly more (74% to 65%); of those centers who have discarded services, the top third tends to have discarded lending filmstrips slightly more (22% to 13%).

Table 36 indicates that released time for users occurs in about 60 percent of the instances and the top third of the centers tends to report released time somewhat more frequently (60% to 52%).

TABLE 35
Services Offered and Discarded

(Number of Responses)	Percentage of Responses			Team Rating of Center	
	Total (236)	"In Group" (73)	"Out Group" (163)	Percent in Top Third (86)	Percent in Lower Third (76)
None	60	36	71	65	74
Lending audiovisual film-strips (school has own)	21	36	14	22	13
Reduced display of media (loss of space)	6	3	7	5	3
Regular evening courses	3	8	1	1	1
In-service courses with credit	3	7	2	1	4
State approved book list, catalog (no freedom of choice)	3	4	3	3	-
Meetings, conferences (lack of space)	2	4	1	1	2
Educational television (funding cut)	1	-	1	-	3
Civil rights work (lack of funds)	1	2	-	2	-

TABLE 36
Amount of Released Time for Center Use

(Number of Responses)	Percentage of Responses			Team Rating of Center	
	Total (275)	"In Group" (79)	"Out Group" (196)	Percent in Top Third (109)	Percent in Lower Third (75)
No time	41	36	44	40	48
Time	59	64	56	60	52
Not specified	21	24	19	24	14
During the day	14	15	13	12	12
Less than one day	8	10	7	6	12
Only for special work-shops, classes	7	6	8	10	3
Two days	5	5	5	5	6
One day	3	1	3	3	2
More than one day	1	3	1	-	3

User suggestion or request is the most frequently occuring reason for offering in-service training (36%). This occurs as the reason twice as frequently in the top third centers (33% to 16%). Among the lower third of the centers, "requested by center staff" or "initiated by supervision" are more frequently stated (table 37).

TABLE 37
Factors Determining Provision of In-service Education Programs

	Percentage of Responses	Team Rating of Center	
(Number of Responses)	"In Group" (77)	Percent in Top Third (33)	Percent in Lower Third (19)
User suggestion, request	36	33	16
Observed user needs	20	21	21
Requested by center's staff	21	22	32
Survey of needs taken	10	9	16
Recommended by center director	9	15	5
Program initiated by supervisors	4	-	10

In table 38 the centers rated among the top third differ from those rated in the lower third in the evaluation of new media. The top third more often uses a combination of staff and users (58% to 35%) whereas the lower third more often has the users involved (52% to 24%).

TABLE 38
Evaluation Procedure of New Media

	Percentage of Responses	Team Rating of Center	
(Number of Responses)	"In Group" (80)	Percent in Top Third (33)	Percent in Lower Third (23)
Staff	20	18	13
Users	40	24	52
Combination of staff and users	40	58	35

The two most frequently used selection procedures for new media are "requests from users and staff" and "approved by staff and specialists. " The "in group" indicates the second method with greatest frequency (34%), whereas the "out group, " probably not as informed, believes that the first method "requests from users" is the most frequently used method (33%). No appreciable differences appear between the top and lower third centers (table 39).

TABLE 39
Selection Procedure for New Media

(Number of Responses)	Percentage of Responses			Team Rating of Center	
	Total (322)	"In Group" (98)	"Out Group" (224)	Percent in Top Third (136)	Percent in Lower Third (100)
Requests from users and staff	31	25	33	33	27
Approved by staff and specialists	27	34	24	27	23
After examination of samples at center	17	11	19	18	15
Chosen from bibliographies by those reviewing for center	8	7	8	7	10
Chosen from bibliographies in reviewing media	6	8	5	5	10
Final decision by center director	5	7	5	3	10
Selection policy sets criteria	3	4	3	4	1
After examination of samples on display at conferences	2	1	2	2	2
Chosen from bibliographies in textbooks	1	2	1	1	2

The user role in selection of new media is mainly one of making recommendations (42%). However, respondents in the "out group" believe that they more often make requests (32% to 16%), and those in the "in group" more often indicate that they encourage user reactions and comments (18% to 9%). No significant differences between the high and lower rated centers were found (table 40).

TABLE 40
Role of Users in Selection of New Media

(Number of Responses)	Percentage of Responses			Team Rating of Center	
	Total (253)	"In Group" (83)	"Out Group" (170)	Percent in Top Third (104)	Percent in Lower Third (82)
Recommendations for specific subject or type of material to be added	42	44	40	37	45
Requests that specific items be added to collection	27	16	32	28	24
Serve on evaluation and selection committees	16	16	17	17	20
Center encourages user reaction, comment	12	18	9	13	9
Users assigned reviews by center staff member	2	5	1	3	2
Solicited through survey of schools in area served	1	1	1	2	-

Users' requests for special or individual instruction were most frequently met with assistance from staff members (87%). Both "in groups" and "out groups" and high and low centers offer the same response (table 41).

TABLE 41
Handling of User Special Requests

(Number of Responses)	Percentage of Responses			Team Rating of Center	
	Total (270)	"In Group" (86)	"Out Group" (184)	Percent in Top Third (109)	Percent in Lower Third (87)
Assisted by staff member (specialist at center)	87	87	87	84	84
Staff member goes to school to work with user	6	5	7	8	6
Referred to another source, if unable to help	3	4	3	4	3
Staff member works through subject supervisors to help user	2	2	2	2	5
Staff member directs material to user in his school	2	2	2	2	2

Table 42 indicates the best way to organize the various media is considered to be integrated classification of all media (58%). The "out group" feels more strongly about integrated classification than does the "in group" (65% to 47%). The "in group" prefers to shelve by type of media (36% to 12%). The lower third of the centers more often prefer shelving by grade level (13% to 2%).

TABLE 42
Best Way to Organize the Center's Various Media

| | Percentage of Responses | | | Team Rating of Center | |
	Total (219)	"In Group" (81)	"Out Group" (138)	Percent in Top Third (80)	Percent in Lower Third (71)
(Number of Responses)					
Classification of all media (media integrated)	58	47	65	64	61
Shelved by type of media	21	36	12	24	18
Shelved by grade level of curriculum	8	3	11	2	13
Test various methods; use most efficient	5	3	7	5	3
Shelved by accession number	3	6	2	4	3
Separate professional collection	2	2	1	-	1
Shelved by publisher or distributing agency	2	2	1	-	-
Shelved by color code	1	1	1	1	1

In table 43 the most frequent type of printed material about the center is "newsletter, bulletin, or memos" (37%). The "in group" indicates distribution of booklets, pamphlets, or brochures more often than the "out group" indicates awareness of such communications (24% to 9%). The "out group" is more aware of acquisitions list distribution (20% to 11%).

TABLE 43
Distribution of Type of Printed Material

(Number of Responses)	Percentage of Responses			Team Rating of Center	
	Total (377)	"In Group" (107)	"Out Group" (270)	Percent in Top Third (154)	Percent in Lower Third (111)
Newsletter, bulletin, memos	37	30	39	38	31
Acquisitions list	18	11	20	17	18
Catalogs and supplements	14	13	14	13	16
Booklets, pamphlets, brochures	13	24	9	11	15
Announcements of special events, workshops	8	7	9	9	9
Manuals about equipment, handbooks	3	6	2	5	1
Bibliographies of recommended media	3	6	3	5	5
Calendar of events	3	2	3	2	1
Place announcements in teachers' union paper	1	1	1	-	4

The most frequent sponsor of the media center in this study was the city (35%). Unexpectedly the "in group" states this is so in 42 percent of the cases, whereas the "out group" states this to a lesser degree (33%).

Table 44 indicates that clear-cut differences in the top and lower third of the centers occur. Centers in the top third are more frequently sponsored by the city (42% to 28%). When the state is the sponsor, there are higher percentages of centers in the lower third (37% to 13%).

TABLE 44
Sponsor of Center

(Number of Responses)	Percentage of Responses			Team Rating of Center	
	Total (273)	"In Group" (85)	"Out Group" (188)	Percent in Top Third (111)	Percent in Lower Third (83)
City	35	42	33	42	28
County	27	24	28	25	15
State	22	19	23	13	37
Elementary and Secondary Education Act funds	11	6	13	13	6
Other specific group	5	9	3	7	4

In table 45 the most frequent immediate space growth plans relate to doubling floor space (23%). The second most frequent item is "plans not formulated because of funding problems" (19%).

TABLE 45
Space Growth Plans during Next Year

| | Percentage of Responses | Team Rating of Center | |
| | "In Group" (43) | Percent in Top Third (26) | Percent in Lower Third (5) |
(Number of Responses)			
Floor space to be doubled	23	27	-
Plans not formulated because of funding problems	19	8	(2)
One new room	12	12	-
Two new rooms	9	8	-
Three new rooms	12	12	(1)
Warehouse added	9	12	(1)
Conference rooms to be added	7	7	(1)
Auditorium to be added	4	7	-
Television studio to be added	5	7	-

Long-term growth plans for space are also most frequently stated in table 46 as doubling space (38%).

TABLE 46
Space Growth Plans during Next Five Years

| | Percentage of Responses | Team Rating of Center | |
| | "In Group" (34) | Percent in Top Third (16) | Percent in Lower Third (10) |
(Number of Responses)			
Floor space to be doubled	38	25	50
Plans not formulated because of funding problems	18	19	10
Three new rooms	12	19	10
Television studio to be added	12	19	-
Warehouse to be added	6	6	20
Conference rooms to be added	6	12	-
One new room	3	-	10
Two new rooms	3	-	-
Auditorium to be added	2	-	-

48

The most frequent response to the question, "What would happen if this center were abolished" was that individual schools would suffer (52%). The "out group" stated this answer more frequently than did the "in group" (58% to 37%).

The "in group" stated more frequently that the schools would be forced to establish individual collections (20% to 9%). No significant differences between the centers rated as the top third and the lower third were found (table 47).

TABLE 47
Effects If Center Were Abolished

(Number of Responses)	Percentage of Responses			Team Rating of Center	
	Total (267)	"In Group" (81)	"Out Group" (186)	Percent in Top Third (105)	Percent in Lower Third (83)
Individual schools would suffer loss of subject enrichment	52	37	58	52	54
Schools would be forced to establish individual collections	12	20	9	9	11
Traditional teaching methods would return	9	9	10	9	11
Communication between schools would end	7	9	6	9	5
Center collection would be scattered	6	1	9	6	7
Collection would remain static, services not available	6	10	4	6	6
Relieve staff; no additional purchases	3	6	2	5	-
Other educational department would carry on	3	6	1	4	2
Only book collection would remain	2	2	1	-	4

Newspapers most frequently gave publicity to the centers (53%) followed by television and radio (30%). The "in group" reported somewhat more awareness of the radio publicity than did the "out group," but both groups indicated about the same awareness of the other two media. The top third centers

49

obtain appreciably more publicity in all three communications
media than do the lower third of the centers (table 48).

TABLE 48
Local Publicity for Center

	Percentage of Responses			Team Rating of Center	
	Total	"In Group"	"Out Group"	Percent in Top Third	Percent in Lower Third
(Number of Responses)	(278)	(86)	(192)	(105)	(94)
Local Radio					
Yes	30	37	27	42	19
No	70	63	73	57	81
Local Television					
Yes	31	30	31	47	22
No	69	70	69	53	78
Newspaper					
Yes	53	56	52	76	31
No	47	44	48	24	69

Most of the centers were rated as either excellent (47%) or
good (43%). The "out group" tends to rate higher than the "in
group" (49% to 36% excellent ratings). Sixty-one percent of
the top third centers were rated excellent whereas 36 percent
of the lower third were rated excellent. These findings offer
evidence of the validity and internal consistency of the visiting
team ratings (which established the top and lower third centers)
as compared to the ratings of the respondents (table 49).

TABLE 49
Respondent Center Ratings

	Percentage of Responses			Team Rating of Center	
	Total	"In Group"	"Out Group"	Percent in Top Third	Percent in Lower Third
(Number of Responses)	(303)	(87)	(202)	(116)	(100)
Excellent	47	36	49	61	36
Good	43	54	40	32	47
Fair	6	6	6	3	13
Poor	1	-	2	1	3
No rating	3	4	3	3	1

Recapitulation of Differences

The interview allows for an analysis of the information as well as the perceptions of the "in group" and the "out group. " As a result of the comparisons, it is possible to indicate where communications have broken down or are in need of improvement.

Similarly, the attempt made to compare the better and the poorer centers, as determined by a combined judgment of visiting teams, furnishes leads which can offer suggestions on how to improve existing centers or work toward setting up model centers.

Differences between "In Group" and "Out Group"

The "out group" reports the use of centers by teachers more than does the "in group" (47% to 40%).*

The "out group" more often than the "in group" states as reasons for using the center "evaluation and review of available media" (25% to 19%) and "media not available elsewhere" (22% to 16%).

The "out group" indicates "better informed about media" as a reason for increased competency more often than the "in group" (28% to 18%).* The "out group" also considers "helped establish criteria for selection" as more important for increased competency of user (23% to 14%).* On the other hand, the "in group" attributes "professional materials have stimulated teaching methods" (21% to 13%)* and "integration of media into class instruction" (17% to 8%)* as more important. More frequently, the "out group" does not answer this question (17% to 3%),* which may be an indication of not having their competency increased.

The "in group" in considering major center goals more often indicates "make teachers aware of wide variety of media to enrich teaching" than does the "out group" (38% to 26%).*

The "out group" considers the one service offering the greatest contribution to advancing the centers' educational service to be the distribution of media (28% to 16%).* The "in group" ranks this service as fourth; training in use of media is ranked first (23% to 9%), *

*Indicates significance of difference between percentages not due to chance.

then "reviews and evaluation criteria for selection"
(20% to 14%), and then " keeping teachers informed"
(19% to 14%).

The "in group" more often than the "out group" reports
"approved by staff and specialists" as a selection procedure for new media (34% to 24%).

The "out group" more often believes that their requests
for specific items play a role in selection (32% to 16%).*
The "in group" believes they more often "encourage
user reactions and comments" (18% to 9%).

Rather clear-cut differences exist between the "in group"
and "out group"as to the best way to organize various
media in the center. The "out group"prefers "media
integrated" (65% to 47%).* The "in group" prefers
to shelve by type of media (36% to 12%).*

The "in group" indicates a distribution of "books, pamphlets, and brochures"more often than the " out group"
(24% to 9%).* The "out group" is more aware of
acquisition lists (20% to 11%).

The "out group" is less aware of city sponsorship of a
center than is the "in group" (33% to 42%).*

If the center were abolished, the "out group" more often
indicates that individual schools would suffer (58% to
37%).* The "in group" more often states that schools
would be forced to establish individual collections (20%
to 9%).*

Differences between Top Third and Lower Third Centers

"Professional materials have stimulated teaching methods"
is more often stated as a reason for increased competency of users by the top third centers (21% to 11%).*
The lower third more often state no answer (21% to 8%).*

The top third centers more often are open additional hours
(63% to 42%).*

The top third centers spend 61 percent to 70 percent of their
time on administration more often than the lower third
(20% to 0%).* The lower third more often spend 21 percent to 30 percent on administration (29% to 6%).*

The top third spends 41 percent to 90 percent of their time
with users more often than the lower third (12% to 31%).*

*Indicates significance of difference between percentages not due to chance.

52

The top third spends more time on supervisory functions
as a major job responsibility than the lower third (23%
to 10%).* The lower third more often assists and in-
structs by telephone (12% to 4%),* or serves as consultants to users (23% to 11%).*

The top third more often considers beneficial additional
education to be "knowledge of curriculum planning"
(26% to 9%)* and "business administration or personnel
management" (19% to 13%). The lower third considers
library experience (25% to 11%)* and audiovisual and
other media retraining (16% to 4%)* as beneficial additional education.

The top third considers the one service offering the greatest
contribution, and as more important than the lower
third, to be training in the use of media (17% to 10%).
The lower third rank distribution of media (23% to 18%)
and "review evaluation, criteria for selection" (24% to
15%)* as more important.

The top third more often plans as a new service "cooperative program with colleges" (18% to 0%).* The lower
third is more often planning "expand use of computer"
(14% to 4%)* and "produce catalog of holdings" (11%
to 5%).

The lower third of the center more often have not discarded
any services (74% to 65%), while the top third have more
often discarded lending filmstrips (22% to 13%).

The top third centers tend more often to report released
time for users (60% to 52%).

With reference to the decisions to offer in-service programs,
the top third more often reports "user suggestion, request" (33% to 16%).* The lower third more often
reports "requested by center staff" (32% to 22%), and
"program initiated by supervisors" (10% to 0%).*

The top third in the evaluation procedure of new media more
often uses a combination of staff and users (58% to 35%).*

The lower third prefer "shelve by grade level of curriculum
is the best way to organize media" (13% to 2%).*

More top third centers are city sponsored (42% to 28%)*
and more low third centers are state sponsored (37%
to 13%).*

The top third centers tend to get much more publicity in
all three communications media. For radio it is 42
percent to 19 percent,* for television it is 47 percent

to 22 percent, * and for newspapers it is 76 percent to 31 percent. *

TEAM EVALUATIONS

The on-site survey teams, which consisted of 73 professionals - media specialists/librarians, curriculum specialists, classroom teachers, college teachers, and administrators, conducted interviews with center personnel and users of the 38 centers surveyed. Their findings are reported in the preceding section of this report (p. 28-53). When the individual team members had concluded their separate interviews, the chairman of the team convened the members of his group to discuss their findings and compile the team evaluation report (see Appendix D). These reports were tabulated and coded and the findings reported in this section. Note that the right-hand column in tables 51-82 represents by actual number, not percentage, the 38 centers visited. Table 50 is an exception in that responses are reported.

The teams rated 16mm films as the most effective audiovisual media in the collections they surveyed (table 50).

TABLE 50
Most Effective Audiovisual Medium

	Number of Responses
16mm films	18
Transparencies	5
Slides	0
Filmstrips (including sound)	4
Microfilm	0
Tapes and cassettes	3
Recordings	0
8mm films (including film loops)	0
Kits (multimedia)	2
Models, realia	3
Pictures, charts, maps	1
Educational TV	1
All effective	1
No answer or vague	7
Total responses	45

The degree to which the collection of media is classified and cataloged is rated good in 16 of the 38 centers. However, another 15 can stand improvement, since these centers are rated either fair or poor. A review of the five centers rated excellent probably will furnish definite leads for Phase II, writing the "Guide" (table 51).

TABLE 51
Rating of Classified/Cataloged Collections

	Number of Centers
Excellent	5
Good	16
Fair	9
Poor	6
No answer	2

When center cataloged collections are rated good or excellent, it is because these collections are organized for ease of use. When collections are rated fair or poor it is either for inconsistent or incomplete cataloging, need of improvement in cataloging, or need of better organization (table 52).

TABLE 52
Reasons for Rating of Classified/Cataloged Collections

	Center's Rating			
	Excellent	Good	Fair	Poor
Nonstandard catalog works well	2	3	-	1
Well related to curriculum terminology	1	1	1	-
Cataloging of nonprint media in process	1	1	-	-
Organized for ease of use	1	5	-	-
Media could be better organized	-	-	2	1
Cataloging inconsistent, incomplete	-	-	3	1
Needs catalog or improved one	-	1	1	1
Needs integrated catalog for all media	-	1	1	1
Only a portion of collection cataloged	-	3	1	1
No reason for rating	-	1	-	-
Total (36)*	5	16	9	6

*Two centers were not rated on this question.

Almost two-thirds of the displays of recently acquired media by centers were rated fair or poor (table 53).

TABLE 53
Rating of Center Display of Recently Acquired Media

	Number of Centers
Excellent	10
Good	4
Fair	9
Poor	14
No rating	1

Differences in center display rating indicate that the better center exhibits are well organized and updated and the poorer center exhibits are not usually previewed, current, or well organized (table 54).

TABLF 5
Reasons for Rating of Center Display of Recently Acquired Media

	Center's Rating			
	Excellent	Good	Fair	Poor
Well organized displays with acquisitions updated	5	1	-	1
Had opportunity to observe, examine displays to determine quality	3	-	-	-
Well done although limited space	2	1	3	-
Quality of display dependent upon selection of media in display	-	2	2	-
Not displayed for evaluation, preview	-	-	1	5
Latest, new additions not displayed	-	-	-	3
Displays set up irregularly	-	-	-	2
Only part of collection displayed	-	-	1	1
Crowded conditions result in few displays	-	-	1	-
Displays not maintained, updated	-	-	-	1
Displays poorly organized, inaccesible	-	-	1	1
Total (37)*	10	4	9	14

*One center was not rated on this question.

About two-thirds of the centers maintain an evaluation file; the rest do not. Of those who do, only slightly more than half had such files rated as excellent or good. In other words, almost half of the centers with evaluation files were rated either fair or poor (tables 55 and 56).

TABLE 55
Existence of Evaluation File for Media Added to Collection

	Number of Centers
Do maintain evaluation file	26
Do not maintain evaluation file	12

TABLE 56
Rating of Evaluation File

	Number of Centers
Excellent	6
Good	8
Fair	5
Poor	7
Total	26

The more persons, especially users, involved in contributing to the evaluation file, the better that file is judged to be. This supports the qualitative research finding that committees of users and staff, rather than only center directors and staff, should conduct evaluations (table 57).

TABLE 57
Reasons for Rating of Evaluation File

	Center's Rating			
	Excellent	Good	Fair	Poor
Both groups and individuals have opportunity to evaluate and recommend	3	3	-	-
File kept only on some materials	1	2	1	3
Users contribute heavily to evaluation file	1	2	-	-
Full access to all materials in permanent evaluation file	1	-	-	-
Inaccessible	-	-	-	2
Few established criteria for evaluation; uneven quality	-	1	1	1
No file; evaluation attached to item	-	-	-	1
File kept for limited amount of time	-	-	1	-
New evaluation form being initiated for all media; new file will be maintained	-	-	2	-
Total (26)	6	8	5	7

Education programs in centers were rated as excellent or good in almost two-thirds of the instances. When so rated, the major reason is "wide variety and quality of workshops." The reasons for poor ratings relate to need for improvement, expansion, or better planning (tables 58 and 59).

TABLE 58
Rating of Center Education Programs

	Number of Centers
Excellent	11
Good	13
Fair	6
Poor	5
No rating	3

TABLE 59
Reasons for Rating of Center Education Programs

	Center's Rating			
	Excellent	Good	Fair	Poor
Wide variety, quality of workshops	4	4	-	-
Description of programs, reactions of staff and users indicate the relative quality	2	2	-	-
Tries to involve, serve every teacher in system	1	1	-	-
Programs based on study of needs, then followed up	1	2	-	1
Group or individual classes offered throughout year	1	-	-	-
No training done at center; no orientation	1	-	1	2
Needs to be expanded, improved; planned better	-	4	4	2
No (or poor) training for users in evaluation, selection of media	-	-	1	-
No answer	1	-	-	-
Total (35)*	11	13	6	5

*Three centers were not rated on this question

The print and nonprint collections tended to be rated rather similarly insofar as fewer than a third of the 38 centers were rated excellent or good. The remaining centers were rated fair or poor (table 60).

TABLE 60
Rating of Print and Nonprint Collections

	Print Collection	Nonprint Collection
Excellent	4	1
Good	12	14
Fair	12	14
Poor	8	8
No rating	2	1

The print collection was rated lower when it was considered primarily to be a professional collection, textbook collection, or inaccessible (table 61).

TABLE 61
Reasons for Rating Print Collection

	Center's Rating			
	Excellent	Good	Fair	Poor
Small collection, limited kinds of media, good quality	2	3	4	1
Establish strong selection criteria	1	-	-	-
Broad representation of current titles; retrospective collection limited	1	-	1	-
Outdated; few current titles; needs weeding	-	4	1	-
Lack of balance in subject matter; not selective	-	2	2	1
Restricted selection to list of recommended titles (state approved)	-	1	1	1
Collection favors particular age group	-	1	-	-
Primarily a professional, textbook collection	-	1	2	4
Inaccessible	-	-	1	1
Total (36)*	4	12	12	8

*Two centers were not rated on this question.

59

The chief reason for poor ratings of audiovisual materials relates to the limited quantity held by centers. The nonprint collection was rated lower when the collection was small with limited kinds of media (table 62).

TABLE 62
Reasons for Rating of Nonprint Collection

	Center's Rating			
	Excellent	Good	Fair	Poor
Large collection; wide variety; strong reviewing program	1	1	-	-
Not wide enough range of kinds of media	-	3	9	4
Evaluation, selection not stable; uneven quality	-	2	-	1
Lack of balance in subject matter	-	2	-	1
Good circulation; hence fewer items available at center	-	2	-	-
Outdated; needs weeding	-	1	1	-
Small collection; limited kinds of media	-	1	4	1
Wide range of materials in most subject areas	-	1	-	-
No nonprint collection	-	-	-	1
No answer	-	1	-	-
Total (37)*	1	14	14	8

*One center was not rated on this question.

The attitude of the "out group" and the "in group" toward the center tended to be rated either excellent or good in most instances. The "in group" (center directors and staffs) had a higher opinion of the center than the "out group." There is not much range of opinion within the occupational classifications of users (table 63).

TABLE 63
Attitude of User toward Center

	Center's Rating				
	Excellent	Good	Fair	Poor	No Report
"In Group"					
Center director	21	12	3	1	1
Center Staff	20	13	1	-	4
"Out Group"					
Administrator	16	17	1	2	2
Principal	17	13	4	-	4
Curriculum specialist	22	10	3	-	3
Media specialist/librarian	22	6	5	2	3
Teacher	18	13	1	1	5

Although the center overall rating is reported to have caused some confusion, the ratings tend to be quite high. Twelve of the 38 centers were judged to be excellent and 19 were judged good (table 64).

TABLE 64
Overall Rating of Center

	Number of Centers
Excellent	12
Good	19
Fair	3
Poor	2
No rating	2

Reasons for high center ratings are staff, services, and user participation. Centers with limited media and in need of integrating their collections could be improved (table 65).

The centers, as judged by the teams, were reported to focus more on collections of media than on training, by a two-to-one margin. The greatest strengths of a center were considered to be staff enthusiasm and ability and good relations with users (table 66).

61

TABLE 65
Reasons for Overall Rating of Center

	Overall Rating			
	Excellent	Good	Fair	Poor
Cooperative, enthusiastic, capable staff	8	4	-	-
Services being offered are wanted, needed, but should be improved	1	5	-	-
User participation, support, and enthusiasm is strong	1	2	-	-
Strong program of in-service courses and consultation	1	1	-	-
Would be better if collection were integrated	-	3	1	-
Weak communications within organization	-	1	1	-
Collection composed of materials from state approved lists only	-	1	-	-
Limited media and subjects covered	-	-	-	2
No answer	1		1	-
Total (36)*	12	19	3	2

*Two centers did not receive an overall rating.

TABLE 66
Greatest Strength of Center

	Number of Centers
Staff enthusiasm, ability	12
Good relations with user	5
Provides service on request	3
In-service training	3
Film collection, circulation	3
Media available for evaluation, selection	2
Processing of materials	2
Media correlate well with curriculum and professional needs of users	2
Well supported, large budget; administrative backing and cooperation	1
Functional quarters	1
Leadership of director	1
Training of media aids, evaluation committees	1
Published listing of recommended materials	1
No answer	1

The greatest weaknesses of a center were considered to be uneven, unbalanced collections and a lack, or poor use, of space (table 67).

TABLE 67
Greatest Weakness of Center

	Number of Centers
Uneven, imbalanced collection	7
Lack of space, or poor arrangement of existing space	7
Lack of funds, or unreliable support	4
Collection not integrated	4
Shortage of professional staff	4
Poor, small, nonprint collection	3
No audiovisual collection	2
Collection not displayed	1
Limited quantity, quality, variety of print media	1
Few media specialists in schools	1
Materials not provided quickly enough	1
Little planning or development of program for center	1
No answer	2

For 22 of the centers there was either limited or no work with community groups. However, seven reported extensive community involvement (table 68).

TABLE 68
Extent Center Staff Works with Community Groups

	Number of Centers
Limited assistance	14
None	8
Extensive community involvement	7
Upon request from community groups	6
Center makes effort to involve community groups	3

The majority of centers have plans for improvement and change. Most of these plans are for more space (table 69)

63

and were likely to be achieved in relation to budgetary conditions (table 70).

TABLE 69
Plans for Change and Improvement

	Number of Centers
Have no plans	5
Have plans	
More space (additions, new building)	20
Computer-assisted instruction	3
Integrate print and nonprint collection; cooperative programs	2
Establish preview area with listening carrels, displays, and viewing area for audiovisual media	2
Employ more media specialists	2
Automated access to collection	1
Enlarge training program, additional workshops	1
Graphics production service	1
In-service training for use of audiovisual equipment	1
Total	38

TABLE 70
Judged Reality of Plans for Change and Improvement

	Number of Centers
Good support	13
Center needs improvement, but has no plans or funding	6
Subject to provisions of funds	5
In planning stages; no approval or funding yet	4
Space available; plans underway	3
Building under construction	1
Funding approved; awaiting bids	1
Center needs improvements; limited budget hinders	1
No answer	4

64

The teams judged the most important improvement needed by the centers to be increased space. Other improvements needed were better organization of collection, integration of print and nonprint collections, and better funding support (table 71).

TABLE 71
Most Important Improvements Needed by Center

	Number of Centers
Increased space	15
Better organization of existing collection	7
Integrate print and nonprint collections	5
Better funding, support	4
Enlarged staff, better guidance needed to meet demands of programs offered	3
Evaluation procedures, criteria	2
More types of media	1
No answer	1

Future financial support seems more secure when it is on the local level rather than when it is on the state level. For example, financial support projected as uncertain and poor is mentioned nine times on the local level but 23 times on the state level (table 72).

TABLE 72
Indication of Future Financial Support

	Number of Centers	
	Local level	State level
Good	12	8
Funds appropriated	2	-
Pending approval of funds	1	2
Support will be maintained, possibly expanded	2	-
Uncertain	1	6
Poor	8	17
Subject to review by new superintendent	-	1
No support	4	-
No answer	8	4
Totals	38	38

Media information obtained from the two mail questionnaires was judged as accurate in 27 instances. Reasons for inaccurate reflections were primarily attributed to changes that had taken place in the interval between the time the center had returned the questionnaires and the on-site survey (table 73).

TABLE 73
Accuracy of Information on Media

	Number of Centers
Was accurate	27
Was not accurate	
Recent weeding	3
Only approximations	2
New material has been added	2
Collection scattered; difficult to obtain	1
Not enough information given on questionnaire	3
Total	38

Of the 38 centers, 22 were judged to have inadequate collections of media to support existing programs. The primary limitation relates to weakness and imbalance of collections (tables 74 and 75).

TABLE 74
Adequacy of Media Collection to Support Program

	Number of Centers
Adequate	16
Not adequate	22

66

TABLE 75

Reason for Adequacy/Inadequacy of Media Collection to
Support Center Program

	Number of Centers	
	Adequate	Not Adequate
No answer	11	3
Too many weak areas; limited, unbalanced collection	-	6
Collection not strong enough to support existing or planned training programs	-	5
Collection does not allow center to function as selection center	-	3
Stronger in print area	1	2
Relates well with curriculum and its development	2	2
Poor financial support	-	1
Better use can be made of a particular type of medium	1	-
Good reviewing, selection standards	1	-
Total (38)	16	22

The audiovisual media equipment is judged as being conveniently located and accessible in 28 of the 38 centers (table 76).

TABLE 76

Convenience and Accessibility of Audiovisual
Equipment

	Number of Centers
Audiovisual equipment is:	
Conveniently located and accessible	28
Not conveniently located and accessible	8
No answer	2

The effectiveness of the collection for student needs was
judged as fair or poor in almost half the centers surveyed.

67

The reasons for the different ratings however are not clear,
at least as far as the codes are concerned (table 77).

TABLE 77
Effectiveness of Collection for Student Needs

	Number of Centers
Excellent	8
Good	7
Fair	15
Poor	2
No rating	6

The staff in 32 of the surveyed facilities was judged to be
familiar with the center's media collection. They were also
considered dedicated and enthusiastic, as well as knowledgeable
(tables 78 and 79).

TABLE 78
Center Staff Familiarity with Media Collection

	Number of Centers
Familiar	32
Not familiar with media collection	4
No answer	2

TABLE 79
Reason for Center Staff Familiarity with Media Collection

	Familiar	Not familiar
No answer	15	1
Dedicated, enthusiastic, knowledgeable	9	-
Familiar with collection; little acquaintance with outside sources, new materials	5	1
Indications are that staff is reasonably familiar with collection	1	1
Lack of integration of audiovisual and print media	-	1
Other	2	-

Only one-quarter of the centers were judged to have a balanced collection. The data in tables 80 and 81 point up the print versus audiovisual media schism that exists in the centers. This schism was detected in the group discussions as well (see p. 77, 81, and 87, "Group Discussions").

TABLE 80
Collection Balance

	Number of Centers
Balanced	9
Not balanced	27
No answer	2

TABLE 81
Reason for Balance/Unbalance of Collection

	Number of Centers	
	Balanced	Not Balanced
Nonprint collection superior to print	-	9
Book collection strong, extensive	5	7
Film collection strong, extensive	-	4
Both areas inadequate	-	3
Nonprint collection unbalanced	-	2
More print than nonprint	-	1
Collection favors particular age group	1	-
Book collection unbalanced	-	1
No answer	5	-
Total (38)	11	27

Many survey teams took the opportunity to offer spontaneous additional comments about the centers. The following list illustrates the variety of comments made. A double asterisk indicates that the item was mentioned three or more times.

**Book selection program is strong
Poor planning
Poor services
No provision for examination of media
Collection favors particular age group or subject
**Poor media evaluation, selection criteria
**Staff willing, eager, enthusiastic, cooperative

69

Center lacks direction, leadership, coordination
Written policy needed for staff personnel
**Policy for center programs needed
**Services and programs should be integrated
**Center should work more closely with curriculum
    development and the established instructional program
**Service well used
More, improved program for training needed
**Center has support and good relationships with the
    administration, board of education, and other super-
    visory groups
Well-developed plans for future
Hours should be extended
Released time for teachers and librarians should be allowed
All media should be cataloged with standard headings
    appropriate to multimedia collections
Staff should offer better reference and consultant services
**Collection needs more subject coverage
**More kinds, types of media needed
**Need for increased funding
Publicity, information on services needed
Should have mobile unit to reach outlying schools in area
    served by centers
**Effective communication with users
Effective reference and consultant services
Collection of media should be current and chosen to support
    curriculum
**Need to evaluate effective use of center and follow-up on
    user needs
**More effective, efficient use of space needed
Collection of media dated; needs weeding
**Circulating review collection should be considered
**No collection set aside particularly for evaluation and
    selection
**Attractive, functional building, rooms
Center's full potential not being utilized by users
Needs more clerical, support staff
**Needs more professional personnel, specialists
Center emphasizes film circulation
Should evaluate all kinds of media
Needs budget planning.

Table 82 presents seven items that were rated by the visiting teams on a four point scale (excellent, good, fair, and poor). Considering only excellent ratings, the centers were rated best on educational programs, recently acquired media, and evaluation files. The combined fair-poor ratings, which indicate that the centers are doing a relatively poor job, occur in recently acquired media, nonprint media, and print media.

TABLE 82
Rating of Services Centers Provide

| | Number of Centers Rated | | | | | |
Item Rated	Combined Excellent/ Good	Excellent	Good	Combined Fair/ Poor	Fair	Poor
Media collection that is classified/cataloged	21	5	16	17	10	7
Recently acquired media	14	10	4	24	10	14
Evaluation file	21	9	12	17	8	9
Education program	24	11	13	14	8	6
Print media	16	4	12	22	13	9
Nonprint media	15	1	14	23	13	10
Effectiveness of collection for student needs	16	8	8	22	17	5

GROUP DISCUSSIONS

Purpose

Since the human interest and the insights of the individual participants in field visits and interviews are often missed if only questionnaire data are gathered, it was decided to find out what the team participants really thought. The method selected to obtain these views and insights was the group discussion technique.

These group discussions served two major purposes - first, to obtain on a face-to-face basis experiences of the team participants at various centers, and second, to serve as a debriefing session where each participant shared experiences

71

with other participants. A side effect was also achieved; for
some, the group discussion was a defusing session.

Procedure

The "Panel Leader's Guide" (Appendix E) was prepared to
obtain from the team members their reactions and attitudes
to briefing, the forms, the value of interviews, the attitudes
of respondents, and, most importantly, to the various centers
visited. In addition, the findings obtained also prepared the
way for transition to Phase II of the project, production of the
"Guide" which is based in part upon the information gathered
in Phase I. Soon after the 38 team visits (in November and
December 1969), seven tape-recorded group discussions of
about two hours duration were held in New York (2), San
Francisco (2), Atlanta (1), and Chicago (2). All 73 team participants were invited to one of the sessions, and, because of
time, availability, and work schedules, 49 persons were able
to attend.

Findings

The following material is reported as findings rather than
results. This is deliberate to emphasize the qualitative nature
of the information obtained, the value of which should not be
underestimated. Such findings may lead to a meaningful understanding of the dynamics involved in the research process, as
happened in these group discussions where attitudes as well as
changes in attitudes were gauged, and often a catharsis effect
was obtained. Such group interaction also may lead to hypotheses
that make future quantitative research more economical and
valuable. Specifically, these findings can help in planning the
methods and steps to be evolved for Phase II of this project.

A content analysis was made where points of view expressed
were studied for repetition or variation from session to session.
When similar themes were independently arrived at, even
though the different sessions had been removed in time and
space and had included different people, they were interpreted
objectively as having significance.

It was found that group discussions had considerable value
when run by a leader who asked only the planned questions
and parried the participants' questions which would reveal
information rather than obtain it. He had to establish rapport,

72

conduct a balanced discussion of opinion differences, recognize and yet not cater to the talkative, disruptive, or excessively critical participant. He also had to get the unduly silent one to talk. In brief, he conducted a true group discussion.

In general, the combination of methods used in visits to centers and the personalities and variations in the centers, as well as experiences of the participants in gathering information, or lack thereof, created group discussions which can be described as rich in catharsis, attitude revelation, and learning experiences.

Team Briefings

    Forty-one of the 49 panel participants reported receiving some form of briefing. These briefing sessions varied in length and substance, and were most frequently limited to interview assignments. In only a few instances did the team chairman actually review the specific questions in each of the questionnaires that formed the basis of the data gathering. It was found that the experience of a previous center visit was most conducive to a better understanding of the procedures involved.

    Interestingly enough, not a single participant indicated that the team chairman referred to the "Panel Leader's Guide" that had been prepared to serve as the briefing outline (see Appendix E). There was also some confusion as to who the team chairman was.

    In a very few instances, the briefing session took place the night before the scheduled visit; in those cases the briefing seems to have been satisfactory.

    The aspect of the briefing session concerned with interview assignments tended to be a function of the advance planning and preparation on the part of the center director. In some cases the center director was fully prepared and provided the team chairman with lists of names. In other cases, lists were not provided and appointments had to be arranged on the spot. Center directors, therefore, tended to have different views about the team visitors.

    Most team chairmen, provided they knew of their assignments in advance, functioned effectively. Only in one instance did a team chairman arrive about one-half day late and leave one-half day early.

Suggestions for Improving On-site Visits

A number of suggestions were made by the participants as to ways in which their on-site visits could have been better planned to give more meaningful results. Some of these suggestions were: a group discussion should be scheduled in advance of the visits; the printed directions should be clearer; the materials should be mailed earlier.

Many participants did not understand why questions they considered inappropriate were asked of certain groups such as teachers or administrators. Other suggestions related to the better selection of centers - some seemed to be totally inadequate or "not centers." Some of the participants felt restricted with the questionnaire and would like to have been given more freedom in their "evaluation."

Although the goal was to have three persons comprise a team, because of the pressures of scheduling this did not always occur. Two-man teams readily reported that their contributions were not as good as three-man teams. The recommendation for any future on-site visits was that there be a minimum of three persons on a team.

Despite the above comments, many participants reported that the visits served the purpose of identifying the center's characteristics. A few were sufficiently sophisticated to recognize the various purposes of the study, such as to establish that educational media selection centers vary in quality, purpose, functions, and the like. Others even recognized that the study was trying to establish the degree of knowledge that various users have about such centers.

Selecting the Respondents

It is not clear whether or not the respondents were randomly selected. Twenty-two interviewers indicated that the respondents were selected at random; twenty-four indicated that they were not. (Three did not know.)

Generally, visiting teams used the procedures that were outlined in the "Team Chairman Guide" (see p. 121-23, Appendix C); that is, they interviewed the name on the

74

list corresponding to the number assigned to the team. This procedure was followed more when the center director provided the lists in advance. As previously reported, some directors did not have such lists ready. Some directors made telephone calls for interviews after the teams had arrived; others arranged for users to come to the center. Sometimes center directors arranged released time for a respondent, thus enabling the interview to be conducted. In other instances interviews were conducted during free periods or after school hours.

A few sophisticated participants preferred to make their own appointments; in rare cases, though they actually avoided the names on the list, they, nevertheless, managed to obtain appropriate interviews in the designated categories by their own selection devices. These team members recognized that even when lists were provided, such users had to be considered "friendly." The inference is that the responses of users may have been more favorable or informed than the responses from all potential users might have been.

Problems of interviewing, especially of members of the "out group," centered around geographic location, accessibility of transportation, and time pressures. Accordingly, it would appear that most interviews conducted with the "out group" were selected for geographic convenience. In a few instances, the option was given to conduct telephone interviews. In every case, with one exception, the telephone interview was judged to be equally informative and as valid as the face-to-face interview. A few participants believed that interviewing members of the "out group" away from the center resulted in better or more valid interviews. They assumed that the interviewee felt freer to talk. Some exceptions to this view were voiced, as for example, interviewing a librarian while on duty or interviewing a teacher in the presence of the class.

Attitudes toward the Questionnaire

Obviously, the opportunity to criticize was increased. The first question in the group discussions on briefing apparently did not encourage the participants to freely criticize their peers in terms of the ineffectual briefing.

The question "How satisfied were you with the questionnaires that formed the basis of your interviews in terms of the answers obtained?" primarily served as a safety valve, even though it was not intended in that fashion. It offered the opportunity to allow many participants to register a variety of complaints and criticisms of both a real and imagined nature.

Many criticisms were offered in terms of the inappropriateness of certain questions. Whether the questions were really inappropriate or the respondents simply did not have the information to answer the questions must be pondered. It appears that what the critics were saying was that, whenever a respondent could not answer a question, the question was inappropriate. This conclusion, of course, is not necessarily justified.

Only a very few sophisticated participants were able to understand that the purpose of the research was to ascertain the kinds of information about various educational media selection centers known by the "in group," (center directors and staff) in comparison with the "out group" (users of the centers or administrators). If these two groups had different levels of information, was it the fault of the questions or the lack of communication between the groups?

Another criticism of the questionnaire was that the same question was asked of all members of the "in group" as well as members of the "out group." Many commented that this was useless repetition, as well as further evidence of inappropriate questioning. Interviews with administrators or principals were especially faulted. Because administrators of the "out group" were not as familiar with the educational media selection centers as they might have been, the interviewers chose to interpret this as caused by inappropriate questions.

Once again, a few participants were able to recognize that the purpose of asking the same questions of the "in group" was to determine the extent of successful communication between staff and users. For example, if users are not familiar with the goals, functions, and services of the center to the extent that the center personnel are, then it is obvious that the centers must more effectively communicate their purposes, functions, and services to the users.

The lack of definition and the confusion of terms used in the questionnaire was also criticized. Once again, a few participants did recognize that by keeping the concepts unstructured and undefined, the researchers could use the concepts that emerged to conduct a more meaningful type of inquiry.

Just as questions were considered inappropriate, so did some consider the selection of centers as inappropriate. This is probably true, but at this early phase in the research it is essential to have a sampling of the wide varieties of centers that now exist, for only at a later stage in the research can it be defined that a center is functional or operational.

Observing the unfolding group discussions, the discussion leader often noted that the participants were more occupied with their role as evaluators rather than as information gatherers. For example, a few would have preferred to write narrative descriptions of the centers they visited, so as not to be hindered by the need for uniformity of data which allowed for comparisons among various occupational groups of respondents.

Attitude of Respondents

The participants generally agreed that the attitude of the respondents toward the interview, as reflected by their answers, was either excellent (22) or good (25). In more than one instance, the favorable attitudes of respondents were regarded as a most rewarding aspect of the visit.

Apparently the inability of respondents to answer some of the questions did not deter the establishing of rapport or the gathering of information. Some respondents were so eager and enthusiastic that they volunteered additional information.

In a few instances a poor attitude existed initially but was ultimately changed, as for example, when an interviewer with a library background interviewed an audio-visual person, and vice versa. When interviewers demonstrated their familiarity with both types of material, and when they indicated no bias, they were able to over-

77

come respondent resistance and establish rapport. If a center director regarded the team visit as a threat, establishing a favorable attitude, initially, was more difficult.

Judged Interview Value

The value of the on-site interview was judged by the participants to be good (27). Ten additional participants rated the interview value as excellent, whereas 12 rated it fair. In other words, a consensus rated the value of the interview as good, even though the questionnaire as a basis of obtaining answers was rated as only fair.

Illustrations of the value of the interview are indicated by the following statements: "Seeing centers, seeing the concept of different persons interviewed toward what the center is supposed to be doing, was great." Another indicated, "The message or role of the center is not getting through to all the people as one moves down the line." Another stated that "The interview allowed you to get an opinion of what the center is doing pretty fast." There also were a number of comments indicating that the interview allowed one to estimate the degree to which the center was personal or impersonal, effective or ineffective.

The interview was also valuable as a learning experience for team visitors. They said they not only learned what to do, but also what not to do. For example, the participants felt that center personnel should be more communicative with users on lower levels. In many instances teachers were not aware of the advantages of the centers; in some cases both the people interviewed and the interviewers reported that their points of view were broadened or changed. These successful interviews undoubtedly resulted from the give and take in a good interview situation.

Personal Benefits or Learning Experiences that Resulted from Visits to Centers

Most team members indicated, with a high degree of sincerity, a valuable learning experience as a result of visiting centers. They now felt better able to

evaluate and improve their own centers because of
the different and better methods of operation which
they had learned. A few experienced reinforced
feelings about the value of the work in which they are
presently engaged.
Several participants reported that many functions from
center to center within even the same state are highly
duplicated and questioned the value of this excessive
duplication. Probably the one function of a center
reported to be duplicated most often with the greatest
expenditure of professional time and talent was the
evaluation of the same instructional materials for
very similar audiences.
It was observed that large and small centers have problems
that require different solutions. Size of the student
population being served and the number of adults
using the individual center would determine, in part,
the amount of funds allocated for staff, collections of
media, training, equipment, and space for a center
program. Probably the Phase II "Guide" will include
recommendations for the minimum support required by
an educational media selection center in these various
areas.
Differences were noted in attitude as well as behavior of
persons who by training, experience, and background
have either a predilection for audiovisual media or an
identification with print. The implication is quite
clear - a media center must do more than recognize
both print and audiovisual materials. Those few centers that have evolved to the point where they have
for all practical purposes two directors, one for audiovisual and one for print, are demonstrating unequivo-
cally that a "house divided shall fall." The schism,
whether it is present or potential, should be faced
and solved. Avoiding serious future conflicts requires
a beneficent and benign view toward these differences.
With reference to other personal learning experiences,
some comments would indicate that a few centers may
have already become so specialized as to prevent
their potential growth into comprehensive educational
media selection centers. Some are overorganized;
others are not organized enough. Some are overcata-
loging and overindexing. One center is cataloging

without the benefit of the books; another had all its media solicited free.

Discussions indicated that there is no standard method of evaluating media. In some centers the director does the evaluation; in others it is done by the staff. Some participants questioned whether center directors should usurp the function of evaluation and suggested that directors be involved more in the function of service and administration than in evaluation. In only a very few situations is the evaluation of media done by committees of users. Apparently the participants believe evaluation should be conducted by committees of users comprising the broadest base. It should always be kept in mind that evaluation must ultimately serve the purpose of advancing and improving the education of students.

The Group Evaluation

Both the qualitative comments and the questionnaire tallies indicate the high degree of acceptance of the group evaluation questionnaire form. In fact it is at this point in the group discussion that many of the team members began to gain insights related to the planned on-site visit. Twenty-three of the participants rated the group evaluation as excellent. Nineteen rated it as good, and only seven rated it as fair. Overwhelmingly, the discussions required to complete the group evaluation were considered extremely valuable. Only a few people considered it restrictive. The majority recognized that the group evaluation form encouraged the integration of the previous interviews conducted by the various team members. As a rule the participants were not involved in a general judgment or "halo" situation. They apparently independently noted each specific question and registered differences in their ratings from question to question.

The group evaluation may best be summarized by one comment: " It made for a more cohesive picture. " There was general agreement that each team member, regardless of his background and interviews, made a contribution to the views of others. When there

80

was agreement, there was no problem, but when there were differences of opinion, the opportunity for full and complete discussion generally resulted in " good consensus. " In a minority of instances, a few persons expressed concern that the group evaluation might result in ratings higher than warranted. The view was expressed that, either because of the "politics of the situation" or friendship between one of the team members and the center director, there might have been a tendency or unwillingness to rate a center too severely.

Probably the high point of the team visit in terms of both value and personal acceptance was the group evaluation. All evidence points to thorough, lengthy, and involved discussions prior to completing the form. It is here that we see a fusion of views and differences of opinion in spite of different backgrounds, differences in interviewing skills, and different persons being interviewed. In only one instance was the group evaluation not a team participation. Generally, the group evaluation resulted in a strong team consensus. When asked if the group evaluation of the center at the close of the visit involved team participation, the immediate and enthusiastic response was generally "very definitely a team effort. " It appears that most teams spent a considerable amount of time in discussing information necessary to evolve the group evaluation.

Another by-product of the group evaluation is the emerging awareness of the really different points of view held by librarians and audiovisual people. It was generally recognized that teams having both types reflected a more comprehensive evaluation. It should be noted that, at least for the present, a schism based on background and training does exist, even though most team members would deny that their own views are biased in this regard. The future success of educational media selection centers will require strong directors who embrace both print and audiovisual concepts. Centers that are represented by two different people, i. e., print and nonprint, or centers whose directors heavily lean toward one of the two lines of media are likely to have difficulties.

Team Comparisons

The participants tended to be uncritical of the characteristics of the various teams at the various centers. Although they felt that the teams were equally good, they also indicated a preference for teams consisting of at least three members - an expert in print, an expert in audiovisual media, and either an administrator or college teacher, so that the expertise would be balanced. The value of a third person on a team was that he not only contributed to the opportunity to obtain more data and presented an additional point of view, but probably and most importantly aided in obtaining a majority opinion whenever disagreement among two people occurred.

Center Comparisons

To the participants who visited two or more centers, it was quite clear that centers differ from one another in philosophy, function, attitudes, services, and collections. Some of the centers function within a very narrow scope, such as providing film deliveries to schools. Others were highly diversified in function. It was at this point in the group discussion that there came the stark realization that an educational media selection center as an entity does not exist, either by definition or by practice. The variations are so great that a generalization about a comprehensive program is impossible. Some centers function primarily in service, some in selection, some in their particular form of evaluation, and a few function primarily as training centers.

It is impossible at this time to discuss the similarities of educational media selection centers. The generalization is that the differences are greater than the similarities. In the future, hopefully, the reverse will be true.

One further point - some centers are presently judged to have potential and others to be totally inadequate. In the future, plans should be made to concentrate on the development of various centers with potential and to correct the inadequacies of the existing centers.

The Training Function

It was noticed after conducting the first two group discussions, that very little information was volunteered on the training function of educational media selection centers. As a result, the panel leader's guide was modified in the remaining cities to ask a direct question about the training function at the media centers visited. Not too surprisingly, it was found that educational media selection centers varied in their training functions as in their services, evaluations, facilities, and the like. The group discussions did yield leads and suggestions as to what to look for. For example:

"The training programs in all three centers I visited were excellent, and they did involve adults from the neighborhood, but mostly teachers and administrators."

"This unit is specifically set up for in-service training of every kind and variety from one-day stands to weeks and months, with a program that is ongoing and planned for years in advance."

". . . had some courses in evaluation and a number of sessions in terms of equipment and materials, and they are doing some in-service training with teachers and administrators on portable videotape systems."

". . . had effective workshops on selection of materials and operation of equipment for the elementary schools that were setting up instructional materials centers. However, there was little being done at the secondary level."

Suggested Major Divisions for a Guide

To familiarize the participants with Phase II of the project and to obtain their ideas, each was asked to suggest independently a number of major parts or categories that would comprise the "Guide to the Development of Educational Media Selection Centers" to improve existing centers or help those planning to establish new centers. Although variations occurred, a number of suggestions were similar from person to person and group to group. It was possible to categorize the various suggestions in the outline which follows:

Categories of Major Suggestions

Purposes, Objectives, and Philosophy (Definition)
Organization and Structure
    Administration
    Relations with other institutions
Program
Policies
Users
    Needs
    Types
    Maximum use
    Group
    Community
Levels or types
    State department
    School system
    Regional centers
    Professional libraries
Center (physical)
    Accessibility, location
    Size
    Space
    Equipment and furnishings
    Hours of operation
    Types of rooms
Selection and Evaluation
    Criteria
    Methods
    By whom
    How frequent
    Committees
    Policy
    Procedures for new acquisitions
Media (Print and Nonprint)
    Kinds
    Balance
    Quantity
    Organization

Material Production and/or Reproduction
Staff and Personnel
    Selection
    Qualifications and standards
    Pattern
    Number
    Job specifications
    Internships
Storage and Retrieval System
    File
    Catalog
    Computer
Budget and Funding
    Assurance
Services
    Types
    To whom
    Degree of emphasis
Training Programs
    In-service
    Workshops
    Courses
Growth Planning
Center Evaluation and Research
    By whom
Relations with Suppliers
Communications and Public Relations

Recommendations for the "Guide"

Following the discussion of these categories, each participant was asked to select one division and list five of
the most important items in that division. The nature
of the responses indicated that there is very little agreement on what these items are. Sometimes it was a
general statement such as "ways of involving system
personnel in evaluation procedures" or "provision for
periodic evaluation of program especially in relation to
its value to teachers and librarians." Sometimes it
resembled a division or a subdivision heading such as
"organization of media for effective evaluation." Sometimes it was a directive such as " begin with giving
services teachers feel they need - expand" or "achiev-

ing real and complete integration of media." At times
the item was stated in the form of a question, i.e.,
"are new materials procured, evaluated, and made
available when they are released?" Other times it was
a brief statement elaborating a division suggested, i.e.,
"short-term internships for intensive training."
Further illustrations would only indicate that these experienced participants generally do not know what these
recommendations should be nor do they agree on their
style. If this is true, then it would be appropriate to
have a "committee of wise men" convene to define
characteristics of guidelines which can be standardized
and established. From the written statements, as well
as the tapes, one must infer that writing the "Guide to
the Development of Educational Media Selection Centers"
will be a most difficult assignment.

Summary

The group discussions successfully served three purposes -
information gathering, debriefing, and defusing.

Team chairmen did conduct briefings for the members, but
generally they were not as comprehensive or meaningful as
they might have been.

The on-site respondents generally were selected from lists
provided by center directors and this method may have produced
"friendly" respondents. Since the research objective was to
obtain information from users leading to the production of a
"Guide," the method used was deemed appropriate.

The interview as a basis for obtaining information was, on
the average, judged to be fair.

Several team members were critical of having been sent to
a specific center, of the assumed inappropriateness of the
questions, and the repetition of questions from one interviewing
category to the next.

A few team members did recognize that a purpose of the research was to obtain comparative information between a center
staff and users, and concluded that the criticism of inappropriateness or repetitive questions may not have been justified.

Attitude of respondents toward the interview was judged as
halfway between excellent and good.

The respondents, both center staff and users, tended to be enthusiastic about the value of educational media selection centers in the educational process.

The interviewers judged the value of the average interview to be good.

Many personal values, insights, and learning experiences accrued to the team members, such as how to plan for improvements in one's own center, what is wrong with some centers, the need for more effective communication with users and potential users, a more objective comparison of their center with others, and a feeling of the usefulness of their work at educational media selection centers.

The team evaluation was rated excellent by almost 50 percent of team members.

Educational media selection centers were found to have great differences in such fundamental areas as function, service, evaluation methods, training, media emphasis, physical facilities, and the like. To conclude that an educational media selection center does not exist as either a prototype or a model would not be an exaggeration.

Probably the most serious problem that could prevent educational media selection centers from reaching their potential is the schism between audiovisual and print people. This is to say that differences in background, training, and experience produce different emphases on kinds of media collections and the ways these are handled. There is little evidence that an attempt is being made to solve the problem other than to split the centers into print or audiovisual parts. In the long run, this will not be a solution at all.

Team members expressed a preference for teams of three persons, each with a different background such as library, audiovisual, administrative, or other experience.

The research method used allows for identifying centers with potential.

A number of major divisions for the proposed "Guide" were suggested that allowed for categorization; the results can serve as a preliminary basis for refinements, reordering, and improvements.

Writing the "Guide" will be a difficult assignment. At present there seems to be little agreement or understanding of what the style should be.

Recommendations

Educators and others familiar with educational media selection centers should be briefed and trained generally in interviewing, and specifically in the use of a questionnaire prior to conducting interviews, if these personnel are to be used in this capacity in this project.

The existing schism between audiovisual and print media should be recognized. People have bias as a result of their training and background which reflects their beliefs. The future of educational media selection centers will depend in large part on leaders in the field who completely and fairly embrace both media.

Since a prototype or model educational media selection center does not exist and the differences among centers are so vast, the urgent need is to work toward an operational definition and to take steps to establish model centers.

3
Conclusions
and
Recommendations

CONCLUSIONS

Very few if any educational materials selection centers, as originally envisioned in the proposal for this study, actually were found to exist. There is at present, in fact, no one model that approximates the ideal. Further, it has been determined that this originally conceived ideal "center" may not, indeed, be the most desirable kind of resource in every situation. The functions of selection and evaluation of media are, however, being performed in many of the centers identified by the study, at a wide variety of levels and effectiveness. The failure to identify even a small number of centers fully performing these functions, which was the central purpose of the study, may thus indicate the need to develop guidelines for a variety of models, rather than for a single model.

Related to these findings is the need for an accepted definition of a center, with implications for this to be considered as one of the early priorities of Phase II in the long-term study.

Perhaps the most significant finding of the investigation thus far is that the differences among the centers are greater than the similarities. These differences are evident in the quantitative data revealed in the tables that report the findings of the two questionnaires and in the team evaluations at the close of each on-site visit. Variety is evident in the analyses of the data on selection procedures, facilities, services, functions of the centers, nature of the media collections, and the numbers of personnel.

When the centers are categorized as top third and lower third, there are differences between these two levels of effectiveness as corroborated by the staff and user interviews and by the team evaluations. The centers in the top third, for example, are much more oriented to user needs, whereas those in the lower third are oriented toward collections of media. There was evidence of closer identification of the staff with users in the top third centers than was reflected by the staff of the lower third centers. Interestingly enough, this finding has been identified by managment studies of effective administrators, as well as by analyses of the effectiveness of media centers serving students in elementary school buildings.

Since the combined judgment of peers is capable of differentiating the quality levels of "centers," it is possible to determine the factors that contribute to effective performance. These are outlined in some detail in the report on the interviews (see p. 27-54, "Interviews"). As further corroboration of this finding, the group discussion of the team visits was able to produce a tentative outline of guidelines for centers, although the team members were unable to agree on what a guideline is!

To put this finding in different terms, Phase I has identified a number of areas of program and policy which have high potentiality for effectiveness and has also identified a few centers which currently possess a high degree of potentiality in these areas of program and policy.

Programs with high potentiality appear to be mostly characterized by flexibility and fluidity of services, by a greater readiness to respond to user needs (and, conversely, to drop ineffective services), as well as by administrative provisions for longer hours of service and for released time for educators to use the centers. Greater accessibility is thus corroborated as an important component of effective services, as were many other aspects of librarianship.

Among the obstacles to effective center programs that Phase I has identified are: a lack of communication with potential user groups or weak programs of communications; lack of an adequate financial base (for example, overreliance on free deposit of media); the great diversity of needs to be met; and the efforts of centers to adapt to this great diversity of needs without the basic resources. It should be pointed out again, however, that real needs do exist and that efforts to meet these needs are being made.

Another important obstacle to effective programs is the continuing schism between audiovisual interests and print-oriented interests, evident in such aspects as insights and understanding of center directors, responsibilities of directors, and the divided collections or collections limited to either print or nonprint media. General inflexibility and slowness to adapt to new concepts are also perceptible obstacles at the present level of development of effective programs.

There is indication in the data that a general area of considerable weakness is attention to policies for building collections and the need for balance, representation of all types of media, and the development of retrospective as well as current collections. The team evaluations rated 60 percent of the collections as either fair or poor. The accumulation of media, rather than the building of collections, appears to have been the general policy. In the development of the "Guide" serious attention will thus need to be given to the matters of financial support and building of collections.

Another finding of particular significance is the real difference between the "in group" and the "out group," the center staff and the adult users, in their perceptions of the centers. The need for improved communications is obvious; equally obvious is the need for consideration of the opinions of the user group in determining functions and services and in setting priorities. The "out group" perceives a center as primarily a specific information source, whereas the "in group" perceives it as a do-good kind of thing, a resource provided primarily for the purpose of helping the teacher to improve his competency. In one sense, the teachers (and other adult users) are saying " you help me to find and use the materials and let me do my job." Furthermore, the "out group" appears to want more integration of media, rather than organization by kind of media. It is not clear from the data whether respondents thought "integration of media" would be achieved by means of shelving, classification systems, or cataloging, (and this may not matter to the user), but the necessity for organization and servicing of media for the convenience of the user, for easy accessibility of " everything on my subject, " are clear. Another confirmation of the importance of this factor is the finding that the lower third of the centers are more conservative and less flexible in adapting to user needs than are the top third centers.

There appears to be an excessive duplication of effort among the centers, especially in the function of evaluating and selection of media. This high degree of duplication has serious implications for planning and development of such centers, as

well as for the writing of the "Guide." The need for management training sessions, especially for administrators responsible for centers, center directors, and other staff; planning
for more effective use of published review and selection aids;
and the development of selection policies in building media
collections for centers are obvious.

Related to this duplication of effort in selection and evaluation of media is the finding that one-third of the centers do
not maintain evaluation files of media. Half of the centers'
media evaluation files are in need of improvement. Such files
were rated higher when users shared in the process of evaluation and selection. Greater consideration of student needs is
also characteristic of the top third centers.

Center programs sponsored by cities were rated in general
as more effective than those sponsored by states. (There
were, however, two states whose agencies did receive a rating
in the top third by the interviewers). Apparently city-sponsored
centers are closer to their users and better serve needs; in
other words, center policies and programs are more effectively
realized at the local level than the state level, according to
users. In the process of writing the "Guide," it will be
necessary to examine more closely the differences between
city-sponsored and state-sponsored centers - what each kind
of center is intended to do, and what it actually does.

An insignificant number of centers sponsored by public
libraries were identified in Phase I; the number of such facilities is too small to provide any specialized findings. This
situation is a marked contrast to the general findings of the
informal survey of examination facilities for new trade books
conducted in the late 1950s by the Publishers Library Promo-
tion Group. It is likely that the tremendous growth of center
facilities serving teachers and other school personnel, rather
than public librarians serving children and young adults, is a
response to two factors: (1) increased use of media with
students in classrooms, libraries, and other places in school
buildings, which has meant that teachers, librarians, and other
adults working with youth needed training in the use of media;
and (2) increase in the kinds of media thought to be appropriate
and effective in educational use, and in the amount of media
published and produced in the several subject areas of the elementary, secondary, and post-secondary curricula.

Finally, there was genuine recognition of the value of these
centers by the "out group," the users. Though the nature of

this value was stated hypothetically, there is dependable evidence that the centers are of benefit to the users.

RECOMMENDATIONS

The foregoing conclusions include many general recommendations to teachers, librarians, professional organizations, the U.S. Office of Education, and other agencies concerned with improving the use of media with adults and students.

The recommendations that follow are specifically confined to this project, not to the educators, librarians, administrators, and others concerned about the evaluation and use of media, but rather to those who will be involved in this project in some way as staff, field and research people, members of advisory groups, and staff in centers in the model or demonstration phase.

The "Guide to the Development of Educational Media Selection Centers" should be written and published as soon as possible. Prior to writing the first draft, it will be necessary to elicit additional information from various media specialists, educators, and allied professionals so that full and accurate information appears in the manuscript. Later it will be necessary to test portions of the "Guide" in specific centers to determine where changes have to be made.

As soon as the "Guide" is published it needs to be implemented - within the scope of this project - in the model or demonstration phase (III) in communities where there is a need for media selection center programs and which have staff and funds to offer such services. In some instances, programs will be built from the ground up; in others, some steps will have been taken and the facilities and programs will have to be enriched, expanded, and improved in other ways. It is anticipated that the places selected for the model phase of the project will reveal a geographic spread and will be in a variety of administrative patterns - public school system, public library system, college or university, and, hopefully, at least one that is sponsored by a

combination of these. Regional and state-level models
also will be considered.

It is important that information about these model or demonstration centers be disseminated as widely as possible.
In addition to the usual periodic reports, a book as well
as a film about such centers is anticipated. The book
would incorporate information from the "Guide" and
case histories of the model centers participating in
this project. It would include specific information
about the activities of individual centers, their staffing
and funding and would describe the similarities and
differences in these and other areas. Portions of the
film would be made in the model centers.

AREAS FOR FURTHER STUDY

The primary plan and work of Phase I was to collect information. In the eighteen months allotted to this phase of the
project it has become evident to the staff, Advisory Committee,
and other professional personnel working on the project that
additional information is needed before a final, effective
"Guide" can be developed to complete Phase II. The following
general areas need to be probed:

Budget

There probably is a relationship existing between the size
of the budget to operate a center and its effectiveness. This
is not to imply that larger budgets necessarily mean greater
effectiveness, but rather that the number of functions a center
can adequately provide are related to the budget. For example,
if the functions of a center are primarily to be a combination
of evaluating and selection services, media acquisition and use,
and training programs, then the question to be decided, based
on budget, is whether all functions should be partially performed, or rather that some functions should be selected and
be more thoroughly performed than others.

Another aspects of the budget relates to the extent to which
federal, state, and local funds are utilized. Probably a combination of funds, and in some recommended proportion, could

result in maximum fulfillment of the center's total function. A total commitment to the concept of effective educational media selection center programs is costly and necessitates long-range expansion and growth plans. These programs or functions have a vital relationship to the use of media in quality education in general. Various responsibilities for education rest at all three levels - local, state, and federal - which means that all three levels must be involved in major decisions, including those about funding. At present the greatest immediate need is to establish the necessary budget requirements for efficient operation.

Further, centers seem to be afflicted with the lack of assurance of continuing funds over a period of time. An area for investigation would relate to determining the effectiveness of a center in relation to its assurance that budgetary appropriations might continue for more than a single fiscal year.

Content and Balance of Media

The information obtained in Phase I indicates a wide divergence of balance in kinds of media materials and range of subject coverage in all media. It is probably advisable to investigate the relationship that exists between (1) the media content and balance within a center and (2) services to users. It appears that staff and director, as a result of their background and experience, tend to favor one type of media over the other rather than consider the needs of the users. Like school libraries or instructional media centers themselves, educational media selection centers reveal that work needs to be done in many areas in the educational system to encourage the use of all appropriate media with students and other patrons. What is needed in this project is more data about the effectiveness of multimedia programs so that implications can be drawn for efficient center programs.

Purchased and Free Media in Centers

Center collections vary in the amounts and kinds of media accepted free of charge from publishers, producers, and suppliers, and purchased. The assumption that purchased media per se are in some way better than free materials should be avoided when an assessment of a collection is made.

95

What may be the case is that media purchased for a center collection are subjected to a more careful professional selection procedure.

However, it is necessary to consider the quality and quantity of media in the center collection in terms of purchased materials versus free materials and relate these findings to the evaluation/selection efforts of the center. Gathering information about the importance of the selection function to the center program as a whole and to the quality of education in the community served by the center should lead to necessary recommendations and policies that include a standard proportion of free to purchased media in a center collection.

Display and Cataloging of Media

Phase I suggested that center users prefer all the media to be integrated, organized, and displayed by subject matter or curriculum area and that center staffs prefer to catalog and shelve according to types of media. The ultimate resolution of this issue requires the establishment of criteria based on the maximum effectiveness of cataloging and classification for the benefit of the user.

The Audiovisual-Print Schism

There are instances in which a bias based on the background and experience of center staff not only separates print from nonprint material, but also affects the attitudes and behavior of the center director. Whether or not separate media collections are maintained, it is important that center directors and staff be trained to recognize the virtues, advantages, and disadvantages of both print and nonprint materials. Further, the continuing proliferation of quality educational materials requires that educators and other center users be made aware of and encouraged to use such new materials, audiovisual and print, as these become available. Users must be taught how to evaluate, select, and use the various forms of instructional media to supplement and compliment each other; that is, they must be shown how to use all media to best fill the needs of their students, and not depend only on the few items with which they feel most comfortable.

Programs that disseminate information about the center - its collection, acquisitions, and services - that provide training in the classroom use of all media, and that involve users as well as staff in the selection and evaluation of media can help provide the means for closing the gap that currently exists. More effective selection and training programs can be achieved if the center collection itself reflects and enhances the integrated use of media in the school curriculum.

Identifying Potential Areas for Development

Phase I established aspects of center programs for potential development and identified centers with these potentials. Future efforts and concentration are required to identify clearly and describe these aspects or components - training, evaluation and selection, organization of collection, distribution of aids in the use of media in the classroom, and other present and potential functions.

Diversity of Educational Media Selection Centers

Phase I established the wide variety and range of such centers. The findings indicate that it may not be possible to establish a single model or prototype center. Rather it might be wise to establish a grid or network that would enable an individual center to develop in accordance with certain needs and objectives as a function of budget, size, staff, and the like. The unresolved question is whether to promote diversity or uniformity. It appears that some diversity is worth preserving and would have value provided that the center exercise the option which would characterize its most effective operation.

Toward EMSC Phase II

Phase I investigated educational media selection centers. The findings clearly indicate that few if any centers exist. Further, the findings indicate that the name "educational media selection center," which essentially suggests a function, may be too narrow. In all probability, the center should serve more functions than just the selection and evaluation of media. In all likelihood it should serve the major needs of the users regardless of whether they are in the school system or in the community at large. Certainly one of the most pressing needs is for provision of education and advisory programs in the evaluation and use of media for center users. This and other recommendations will be included in the "Guide to the Development of Educational Media Selection Centers," which is planned for completion in 1971.

Appendixes

Appendix A—First Mail Questionnaire

SENT TO:

Educational Media Selection Centers Project

NATIONAL BOOK COMMITTEE, INC. ONE PARK AVENUE, NEW YORK, N.Y. 10016 (212) 689-8620

Executive Advisory Council

Chairman:
MASON W. GROSS
Rutgers, The State University
of New Jersey

ELENORA ALEXANDER
Houston Independent School District

ARTHUR BRODY
Bro-Dart Industries

O. L. DAVIS, JR.
University of Texas at Austin

ROBERT C. GERLETTI
Los Angeles County Schools

ALVIN J. GOLDWYN
Case Western Reserve University

FRANCES HENNE
Columbia University

FRANCES K. JOHNSON
University of North Carolina
at Greensboro

CARL L. MARBURGER
New Jersey
State Department of Education

MOST REVEREND
JOHN B. McDOWELL
Diocese of Pittsburgh

A. EDWARD MILLER
The World Publishing Company

FRANKLIN PATTERSON
Hampshire College

HAROLD W. TUCKER
Queens Borough Public Library

THEODORE WALLER
Grolier Educational Corporation

Project Director

JOHN ROWELL
Case Western Reserve University

Project Coordinator

M. ANN HEIDBREDER
Staff Associate
National Book Committee

100

The National Book Committee, Inc., under a grant from the U.S. Office of Education, is conducting a nationwide study of educational media selection centers.

Ideally, such a center makes available to educators and other adults a wide variety of instructional materials—print and audiovisual—for examination and review prior to selection and purchase for use with children and young people.

1. A center is administered by media specialists who assist *adult* patrons in evaluating materials, and who conduct or arrange in-service training programs for professional educational personnel in the selection and use of instructional materials.

2. A center does *not* sell or take orders for the materials in its collection, and circulation of any part of the collection is normally limited to short-term evaluation and demonstration purposes.

3. A center may be attached to or administered by a local school district, a combination of school districts, a state department of education, a public library, a college or university, or a non-profit education-related agency or organization.

The purposes of this first phase of the study include the identification of agencies and programs which offer one or more of the facilities and services described on page four.

Future analysis of the collections, procedures, administration, expectations, limitations, and problems of these agencies will provide information which, in turn, will offer viable blueprints to the agencies themselves in improving and extending their services and for others who may wish to establish educational media selection centers.

We are contacting you in this preliminary location-identification survey on the basis of information received from the U.S. Office of Education or your state department of education which indicated that through local, state, or federal programs you may be offering *one or more components* of a selection center. We would appreciate your cooperation in completing this brief form and returning it in the enclosed, stamped and addressed envelope by January 27, 1969. A second copy is included for your files. All correspondence and requests for additional copies of this questionnaire should be directed to the project at One Park Avenue, New York, N.Y. 10016

Thank you for your cooperation.

John Rowell
M. Ann Heidbreder

Note: Please read the descriptions on page 4 before answering the questions on pages 2 and 3.

I.   Name of director of selection center _____

     Name of selection center _____

     _____

     Address of selection center _____

     _____

     Telephone number: Area Code _____ / _____ / _____

II.   Name of respondent (if different from director) _____

     Title _____

     Name and address of organization or agency sponsoring selection center _____

     _____

     _____

     Telephone number: Area Code _____ / _____ / _____

III. Check categories which most accurately describe your organization:

     A. Type: ☐ public school   ☐ non public school   ☐ college/university   ☐ public library

            ☐ other (please specify) _____

     B. Description of area served: ☐ state   ☐ regional or intermediate

                               ☐ county   ☐ local

     C. Number of schools: _____ OR size of populations served: _____

IV. Check grade level of materials which is most nearly inclusive of your selection center's collection (check all applicable):

          ☐ elementary   ☐ secondary   ☐ post-secondary

     Number of professional media personnel assigned to selection center (audiovisual specialist, curriculum specialist, librarian, media specialist):

          A. full time _____

          B. part time _____

V. Checklist of characteristics (check all that apply):

    A. Administration of selection center:

        1. Source of funds by approximate percentage (for last reported fiscal year):

            _____ local district _____ state _____ federal _____ private (e.g. foundation) _____ none

        2. Availability of access: ☐ during school day   ☐ in addition to school hours

                              ☐ by appointment   ☐ no appointment needed

    B. Materials in selection center for inspection (check those categories of media available in your center):

        1. ☐ Print materials, except for textbooks

        2. ☐ Textbooks

        3. ☐ Audiovisual materials (except for 16mm film)

        4. ☐ 16mm film

        5. ☐ Programmed instruction of any sort

        6. ☐ Professional and/or curriculum materials

        7. ☐ Other (please specify) _____

    C. Services offered to adults by selection center:

        1. In-service training: ☐ regularly scheduled   ☐ not scheduled   ☐ scheduled on request

        2. Consultant services by selection center staff: ☐ in-center   ☐ field

        3. Use of materials collection:

            ☐ in-center *only*   ☐ limited circulation   ☐ unlimited circulation

        4. Other services (please specify) _____

VI. Check here ☐ if within your administrative unit there is no selection center, or component thereof, of the kind described in this survey.

VII. Comments (use additional sheets if necessary): _____

Please return this form to:

Educational Media Selection Centers Project
The National Book Committee, Inc.
One Park Avenue, 18th Floor
New York, New York 10016

1. THE EDUCATIONAL MEDIA SELECTION CENTER

For the purposes of this study, educational media selection centers are those agencies which provide *one or more* (not necessarily all) of the following services relating to the examination and review, selection and/or use of printed and/or audiovisual materials *by educators and other adults (not students)*.

  a. Non-profit local, regional, or state level collections of instructional materials made available to teachers, curriculum specialists, school and public librarians, audiovisual specialists, media specialists and others interested in previewing educational media appropriate to elementary and secondary schools.

  b. In-service training or consultative programs conducted by a professional staff in the qualitative criteria for selection of suitable instructional materials.

  c. In-service training or consultative programs administered or conducted by the educational media selection center staff in the use of instructional materials with students.

This is *not* a study of school libraries, instructional materials centers, learning resource centers and the like, which are established and administered for use by *students*.

2. THE NATIONAL BOOK COMMITTEE, INC.

Founded in 1954, the Committee is a private, non-profit, tax-exempt organization concerning itself with research and development projects involving multi-media communications utilization and the dissemination of public information regarding these projects.

In addition to administering the annual National Book Awards and sponsoring the National Library Week Program, the Committee has conducted projects and studies for the following agencies: Office of Economic Opportunity (The VISTA Book Kit Project); the Community Action Program (Neighborhood Library Centers and Services report); the Agency for International Development; the National Advisory Commission on Libraries; the National Association of Educational Broadcasters; the National Foundation on the Arts and Humanities; The Fund for the Advancement of Education; and the Council on Library Resources, among others.

The Committee is governed by a 200-member National Board and an Executive Committee whose officers are: Mason W. Gross, President, Rutgers, The State University (New Jersey); Frederick B. Adams, Jr., Director, Morgan Library; William Bernbach, Chairman and Chief Executive Officer, Doyle Dane Bernbach, Inc.; William I. Nichols, Senior Consultant, *This Week* magazine; and Bernard Barnes, retired Vice-President, *Time,* Inc.

GPO 868-691

104

Apprendix B—Second Mail Questionnaire

I. This is the second part of a two-part written survey being conducted by the Educational Media Selection Centers Project of the National Book Committee, Inc., under a grant from the U.S. Office of Education.

For the purposes of this study, educational media selection centers are those agencies which provide *one or more* (not necessarily all) of the following services relating to the examination and review, selection and/or use of printed and/or audiovisual materials *by educators and other adults (not students):*

    a. Non-profit local, regional, or state level collections of instructional materials made available to teachers, curriculum specialists, school and public librarians, audio-visual specialists, media specialists and others interested in previewing educational media appropriate to elementary and secondary schools.

    b. In-service training or consultative programs conducted by a professional staff in the qualitative criteria for selection of suitable instructional materials.

    c. In-service training or consultative programs administered or conducted by the educational media selection center staff in the use of instructional materials with students.

This is *not* a study of school libraries, instructional materials centers, learning resource centers and the like, which are established and administered for use by *students.*

On the basis of an analysis of your response to this Project's first survey, your agency tentatively has been identified as qualifying in one or more of the component areas as an educational media selection center. To enable us to define a more precise profile of your agency, we are requesting additional information in this questionnaire.

Some of the questions asked here are not applicable to every agency being surveyed. It is important, however, that we develop a complete description of the centers included in this study. For this reason, we ask that you respond to every question, and that you note NA (not applicable) in any section which is not relevant to your situation.

We appreciate your continued cooperation by completing this form and returning it in the enclosed stamped addressed envelope by June 18, 1969. A second copy is included for your files. All correspondence and requests for additional copies of this questionnaire should be directed to the Project at One Park Avenue, New York, N.Y. 10016.

May 29, 1969

                                        John Rowell
                                        M. Ann Heidbreder

II. COLLECTION. Please estimate total holdings (purchases, gifts, and/or loans) in each type of instructional media and equipment and place number in appropriate blank.

A. Current inventory of *instructional materials:*

1. Hardbound books other than textbooks, professional books, or curriculum guides _____

2. Paperback books of any type _____

3. Textbooks (except programmed texts) _____

4. Professional books _____

5. Curriculum guides _____

6. Periodicals _____

7. Programmed instruction (any format) _____

8. Other printed instructional materials (e.g., documents, musical scores, etc.) _____

9. Photographs, pictorial or graphic works _____

10. Art prints _____

11. Study prints _____

12. Maps (not transparencies) _____

13. Charts _____

14. Globes _____

15. Filmstrips (sound and silent) _____

16. Slides _____

17. Disc recordings _____

18. Tape recordings _____

19. Transparencies _____

20. Films—16mm _____

21. Films—8mm _____

22. Kinescopes _____

23. Video tapes _____

24. Microfilm _____

25. Realia _____

26. Reference books (encyclopedias, dictionaries)

27. Others (please specify)

_____ _____

_____ _____

_____ _____

B. Current inventory of units of audiovisual equipment:

1. Filmstrip (or combination film-strip-slide) projectors _____

2. Slide projectors _____

3. Filmstrip viewers

4. Film projectors–16mm

5. Film projectors–8mm

6. Disc record players

7. Tape recorders and players

8. Television receivers

9. Videotape recorders

10. Overhead projectors

11. Opaque projectors

12. Microprojectors

13. Micro-readers

14. Micro reader-printers

15. Others (please specify)

III. PERSONNEL. Please give current number of employees in the appropriate blank.

	Full-time	Part-time equivalent
A. Librarians		
B. Audiovisual specialists		
C. Media specialists (combined librarian and audiovisual specialist)		
D. Clerks		
E. Audiovisual technicians		
F. Volunteer assistants		
G. Other media selection center personnel, e.g., curriculum specialists, classroom teachers, etc. (Please specify)		
H. Other (please specify)		

IV. FACILITIES. Please indicate (X) in the columns below whether or not your media selection center's facilities provide space for the functions and activities listed. Where possible, please estimate the size of each area.

	Yes	No	Approx. no. of square feet of floor space
A. Open shelving area(s)			
B. Reading room(s)			

	Yes	No	Approx. no. of square feet of floor space

C. Group viewing and listening area(s)

D. Individual viewing and listening area(s)

E. Materials production area(s)

F. In-service training class-room(s)

G. Materials processing area(s)

H. Others (please specify)

_____

_____

_____

V. FUNDING. Please estimate your expenditures to the nearest dollar *for instructional materials and audiovisual equipment* (combined) for the indicated fiscal years according to the sources of funds. Your Fiscal Year runs from _____ (month) to _____ (month). Please indicate (x) in the following box if you wish to have this information kept confidential. ☐

	Local	State	ESEA II	ESEA III	NDEA III	Other (Specify source)
FY 1965	$	$	$	$	$	$
FY 1966	$	$	$	$	$	$
FY 1967	$	$	$	$	$	$

VI. FREE MATERIALS AND EQUIPMENT. If your center receives gifts or loans of instructional materials and/or audiovisual equipment from publishers, producers, manufacturers, dealers, etc., what is the proportion of these gifts or loans to the *total collection of each item* listed below? Please indicate (X) in the column that most closely approximates the proportion. If you receive no gifts or loans of a particular item, leave all columns for that item blank.

	Less than half	Approx. half	More than half

A. Instructional Materials

1. Hardbound books (exclusive of textbooks and reference books)

2. Textbooks

3. Reference books

108

	Less than half	Approx. half	More than half		
4. Paperback books					37 ☐
5. 8mm films					38 ☐
6. Filmstrips					39 ☐
7. Slides					40 ☐
8. Recordings (all types)					41 ☐
9. Transparencies					42 ☐
10. Maps (not transparencies					43 ☐
11. Charts					44 ☐
12. Globes					45 ☐
13. Microforms					46 ☐
14. Art prints					47 ☐
15. Study prints					48 ☐
16. Others (please specify)					
_____					49 ☐
_____					50 ☐
_____					51 ☐

B. Equipment

	Less than half	Approx. half	More than half		
1. Filmstrip (or combination film-strip-slide) projectors					52 ☐
2. Slide projectors					53 ☐
3. Filmstrip viewers					54 ☐
4. Film projectors—16mm					55 ☐
5. Film projectors—8mm					56 ☐
6. Disc record players					57 ☐
7. Tape recorders and players					58 ☐
8. Videotape recorder systems					59 ☐
9. Television cameras					60 ☐
10. Television receivers					61 ☐
11. Overhead projectors					62 ☐
12. Opaque projectors					63 ☐
13. Microprojectors					64 ☐
14. Micro-readers					65 ☐

	Less than half	Approx. half	More than half
15. micro-reader-printers			
16. others (please specify)			

VII. USE MADE OF CENTER.

A. Please give the approximate number of people in each of the groups identified below who, during a one month period, use (a) your collections of instructional materials and audiovisual equipment and, (b) your advisory services and programs.

	(a) *Collections*			(b) *Services*		
	Little or no use	Moder-ate use	Heavy use	Little or no use	Moder-ate use	Heavy use
1. By librarians, audiovisual specialists, or other media personnel:						
2. By classroom teachers:						
3. By curriculum specialists, school admin-istrators, or other adults:						

B. In general, what type of instructional media seems to be most in demand for pre-selection examination by your adult patrons? Select one of the four items below which most nearly describes your situation and place an X in the box next to it.

1. Printed materials ☐

2. Audiovisual materials ☐

3. About the same for 1 & 2 ☐

4. Not possible to determine ☐

C. Please indicate (X) in the box the approximate number of formal in-service training programs for teachers, librarians, audiovisual specialists, or other adults conducted *annually* by your center (either in the center or elsewhere):

none	1-9	10-24	25-50	50+
☐	☐	☐	☐	☐

110

D. Please indicate (X) in the boxes below the nature of your services to teachers, librarians, audiovisual specialists, or other adults (either in the center or elsewhere):

1. Advice to individuals ☐   27 ☐

2. Workshops for special groups (e.g., subject specialists, grade level specialists, etc.) ☐   28 ☐

3. Evaluation of current media ☐   29 ☐

4. Retrospectice evaluation of media ☐   30 ☐

5. Other (please specify) ☐

_____   31 ☐

_____   32 ☐

_____   33 ☐

VIII. SITE VISIT.

A. Would you be willing to receive a visiting team of two or three educators to observe your center in action? Please indicate (X) in the box below.   34 ☐

    1. Yes ☐   2. No. ☐

B. If you are willing to receive a visiting team, please indicate in the box below which time of the year such a visit would be most convenient for you.   35 ☐

    1. Summer 1969 ☐   2. early Fall 1969 ☐

IX. Please add any additional information which will contribute to this profile of your media selection center. Attach additional sheets if necessary.

Appendix C

KIT OF MATERIALS

for

ON-SITE

SURVEY TEAM VISITS

Fall 1969

TABLE OF CONTENTS

INTRODUCTION TO KIT OF MATERIALS FOR TEAM MEMBERS

To: Members of the Survey Teams for the EMSC Project

This is an open letter from the members of the Executive Advisory Council and the staff to the individuals who have agreed to conduct the on-site visits for Phase I of this project. It offers general background information about the project to date and some suggestions about your visits to the centers.

This study will collect information about media evaluation and training facilities of centers. We have contacted these centers previously. In your kit are copies of two completed questionnaires returned by the center you will visit. The first questionnaire had one primary purpose: to identify those facilities with sufficient collections and programs to warrant completing the comprehensive second questionnaire. Information on the second questionnaire about the collections of media and equipment should help you in conducting your interviews.

From the second questionnaires we selected a sample of the kinds of centers to which we have assigned teams for personal evaluations. Very little attempt was made in the questionnaires to obtain information about the training programs being conducted in and through the centers. Team members will collect the bulk of this data. The two completed questionnaires in the kit should be studied thoroughly before the visit to the center.

Personal visits to the centers selected are essential. No matter how good something sounds on paper, evaluation by informed surveyors completes the total picture. Basically the purpose of your visit is to report which centers, or program components are, in your opinion, educational media selection centers. The questionnaires in this kit have been designed to help you acquire and convey this information as efficiently as possible.

In this kit you will find a group of questionnaires to be used in your interviews with the following personnel:

A. Center director
B. Center staff
C. Curriculum specialist
D. Classroom teacher
E. Media specialist/librarian
F. Administrator
G. Principal

Two extra sets of these questionnaires have been provided. The questionnaires in the kit are to be used for your note taking during the interviews. On one of the sets of extra questionnaires please record your edited rewriting of each of these interviews. The other set is for your files. If you are able to interview more than one person in a category--especially curriculum specialists, teachers, media specialists/librarians or principals--please have extra copies of the appropriate forms made at the center. All of the questionnaires for personnel to be interviewed are printed on different colors of paper. Please be sure that all the colored sheets are returned to the Project Coordinator.

Individuals in each category who are to be interviewed will be made up of persons in the various categories, i.e., teachers, librarians, etc., who have visited the center. These lists will be drawn up by the center director and given to the chairman of your team. The team chairman will begin by selecting the person on the list whose rank corresponds with the number assigned to the team by the Project Staff. Each team has been assigned a number from 1 to 4, and each team will begin its selection of persons to be interviewed in categories C, D, E, F, and G by contacting the name on the list that has a rank that corresponds to the number assigned to your team. For example, if your team is assigned the number "2," then you would contact the second name on the list in each of the categories. If that person on the list does not result in an appointment, then take the next person on the list. Continue this procedure until at least one person in each category has been contacted and an appointment has been arranged.

The team should meet as a group before the site visit and interviews are begun. It is important that all team members have the same orientation to the project and to the site visit.

114

They should not duplicate each other's efforts nor should a respondent be put in the position of having to answer the same questions several times to different team members.

It is preferred that face-to-face appointments be made for those persons assigned to you. In the event that face-to-face interviews cannot be completed within each category, then you will be permitted to conduct a telephone interview. Regardless of whether it is a face-to-face or a telephone interview, please contact the respondent in advance by telephone to make an appointment. Always introduce yourself, explain the purpose of your visit, and tell the respondent how much help he would be giving the project if the appointment were granted.

If it is not possible for you to interview any of the persons assigned to you, please mark "NP" (for Not Possible) on the sheets designed for that category of personnel and return them with your completed sheets. If one or more categories of personnel we have identified do not use the center or have no responsibility for it, mark "NA" (for Not Applicable) on these sheets and return them. On the interview questionnaires (P) means team member should ask probing questions.

Following the survey questionnaires is the Group Evaluation which is to be completed by all the members of the team after they have completed and edited their interviews. Time or other factors will probably make it necessary for the team members to interview and evaluate the centers and collections separately to make the most effective use of the amount of time at their disposal. After the teams have completed their work they should meet as a group to evaluate their findings and to complete the Group Evaluation form.

We asked Professor Mary V. Gaver of the Rutgers University Graduate School of Library Service (New Jersey), to help us suggest some steps to be taken in developing a critical attitude toward the center visited. Her recommendations are as follows:

1. A common understanding of the objectives of the on-site evaluation (and the project)

    Each member of the team should study both completed questionnaires, the project brochure, and the materials in this kit pre-

115

pared for the on-site evaluation. One
member of the team should lead a brief discussion of these concepts to be sure that
all members understand them.

2. Agreement on definition of terms

Team members should discuss the factors to
be evaluated, both qualitative and quantitative, to be sure that the team as a whole
is applying the same standards. For instance,
members should agree in general about the
nature of a "good" training program and a
"poor" one; they should agree about the media
and equipment needed for an "effective" media
selection program for adults using the center.

It is impossible to define these terms or
set standards here. Members of the team should
"agree to agree" about them. If definitions
or standards evolved by the team seem to
differ from those stated or implied in information about the project or in the questionnaires in this kit, please make this clear to
the Project Coordinator in a covering letter
when you return the completed questionnaires
from this kit.

3. Each member of the team should maintain a constant
critical level

There may be a temptation to become more critical
as the period of evaluation proceeds. Please try
to keep your attitude at the same level of criticism
throughout the visit.

4. Objectification of criticisms

As you identify areas of weakness and/or strength,
be sure to document your judgments--that is, cite
objective evidence for your judgments about strengths
and weaknesses.

5. Recognition of range of individual examples

If the center being evaluated exists at present
generally at a low level of effectiveness (or with
most examples skewed toward the bottom of the normal
curve)--as may fairly be presumed in this case--it
is especially important to do the following:

    A.   examine each example of all the cri-
         teria set by the planners; and

    B.   consider each example in terms of the
         clarity and feasibility of the objectives
         set for it by the staff and individuals
         responsible for administration of the
         center;

    C.   determine to what extent the center is
         achieving the goals set for it.

Professor Gaver has helped us to develop some general
guidelines about the collection in a center, too. In addition to the definition of an educational media selection
center of page one of the second, comprehensive questionnaire, we suggest that an ideal center collection should
meet most or all of the following criteria. These are not
considered criteria for most of the centers to be visited;
they describe optimum situations, probably rarely found.

1. The center staff should prepare and periodically
    revise a policy for the establishment and develop-
    ment of the collection covering those aspects
    indicated below which reflect the objectives set
    by the governing body (those ultimately respon-
    sible for the administration of the center). This
    should be a written statement developed by the
    staff and representatives of the educators, media
    specialists/librarians, and other adults in the
    community serving youth, and approved by the
    administration.

2. The collections should be professionally
    selected and purchased for the most part
    to cover all grade levels from pre-school
    through grade 12. It should be a broad

collection of recommended media, not just
those provided free of charge by the pub-
lisher or producer;

3. The collection should provide both a retrospective and a current selection of media
   for examination, evaluation and training of
   adults. New needs of students and new
   changes in the curriculum need to be judged
   and met with all available media, not just
   recent materials or those tailored to a
   particular area of study;

4. The collection should provide a full range
   of print and non-print media for all grade
   levels. Kinds of media are listed on page
   two of the second, comprehensive questionnaire, II. COLLECTION. A. Current
   inventory of instructional materials.

5. The center should contain equipment needed
   to view and hear the non-print media and to
   demonstrate potential methods (and difficulties) of using the most effective combination of media and equipment in the instructional program;

6. The collection should include the whole range
   of subjects of concern to children and young
   adults. (It is assumed that an ideal center
   would serve school and public library needs.)
   In the collection should be the following
   items, in addition to materials designed for
   students: up-to-date collection of textbooks,
   workbooks for students and teachers, programmed textbooks, curriculum guides, and the
   like. The collection should include materials
   in special or problem areas such as foreign
   language materials for FLES programs, black
   heritage or black studies programs, remedial
   reading for all age levels. Funding of the
   collection should be sufficiently flexible
   to permit rapid acquisition of such materials.

7. The collection must be bibliographically organized

so that media can be used effectively. Media very recently acquired may be displayed separately in some cases. Print and non-print media should be organized so that all media on a subject can be easily identified for examination and evaluation;

8. The collection should include the full range and scope of reference volumes, bibliographies, and selection aids appropriate to the philosophy and policies set for the center. Current catalogs from publishers, producers, manufacturers of equipment and furniture, and appropriate service agencies should be available.

9. The scope of the collection should be sufficiently broad to accomplish one of the essential goals of an educational media selection center--comparison of versions, editions, series, newly published and produced materials with those available in the past. The center should maintain a file of written evaluations of media, which should include retrospective comments about the effectiveness of the use of the items in the instructional program.

Please remember that the nine paragraphs above are an attempt to describe the collection in an ideal center. It is unlikely that a substantial number of such centers exists today so very likely you will be evaluating components of the ideal, rather than a full-fledged educational media selection center as we have envisioned it here. As you study the collection, please attempt to verify the data submitted on the comprehensive second questionnaire in a general way. In addition, please evaluate the collection as it relates to the following items:

A. the program conducted by the center;

B. the personnel who use the center;

C. the size and nature of the population of adults for whom the center is intended, and the size and nature of the student population of the community expected to benefit from the total educational program;*

*Chambers of commerce might supply this information.

119

D. number of years the center has existed;

E. strengths and weaknesses of instruction
   in various subject areas.

We are grateful to you for agreeing to make this on-site survey and hope that we have anticipated questions you might have about the entire project and especially about Phase I and this portion of it. If you have other questions or comments, please write or telephone me at the National Book Committee office in New York. (212--689-8620).

Thank you.

M. Ann Heidbreder, Project Coordinator
Educational Media Selection Centers Project

Team Chairman Guide

1. Review the two questionnaires previously completed by the Center which are in your kit.

2. Establish randomness of selection for interviews in the various categories. The center director will provide lists of names of persons who have visited the center in the various categories who have used the center (i. e., teachers, librarians, etc.). The method suggested is as follows: Each team has been assigned a number such as 1, 2, 3, or 4. The team will begin the selection of categories C, D, E, F, and G by contacting the name of the list that has a rank that corresponds to the number assigned to the team. For example, if your team were assigned the number 2, then you would contact the second name on the list in each of the categories. If that person on the list does not result in an appointment, then take the next person on the list. Continue this procedure until at least one person in each category has been contacted and an appointment for an interview has been arranged. Your team has been assigned the number _____ .

3. Review the various questionnaires to be used by the team.

4. Assign various tasks to the team:

   A. Interview with center director - to be conducted by the team chairman
   B. Interview with center staff
   C. Interview with curriculum specialist
   D. Interview with classroom teacher
   E. Interview with media-specialist/librarian
   F. Interview with administrator
   G. Interview with principal
   (Allow for the possibility of conducting telephone interviews with persons in categories C through G.)
   H. Evaluation of media collection
   I. Evaluation of equipment collection
   J. Evaluation of space and physical plant of center

5. Instruct members of your team to take complete notes

even if the remarks made do not seem relevant at the time. The digressions and comments made by the respondent may prove to be important later when the interviews are being edited or when comparing notes with the other team members during the final group evaluation.

6. Have the team members edit and rewrite each interview from notes immediately after each interview has been completed.

7. When a question asks for samples of documents, i. e., a job specification, and it is furnished, record "See Exhibit 1" as part of your answer. Number the document in corresponding fashion and attach it to your interview. Continue to number any samples furnished in consecutive order.

8. All members of the team are asked to assume a dual role during the site visits. While conducting the assigned interviews please limit your conversation primarily to specific questions listed on the questionnaire. Try to politely avoid answering questions asked of you and as best you can refrain from offering any information. The best way to obtain and maintain rapport is to place yourself in the role of seeking information from the person you are interviewing (i. e., this person is the authority).

9. In communicating with the people you interview, try to play down your role as an evaluator of the center. Since most people do not like to be evaluated, your interview will prove to be richer in its findings if you present yourself as an information seeker.

10. Convene the team members for the group evaluation. Please discuss each question and record one answer. The group evaluation is important because it will furnish the material from which the Guidelines for a model center will be written.

11. When Sections IV and V are completed, remove all of the colored sheets from the binder and staple together all the sheets of one color in numerical order. The sheets for the center director would be stapled in one lot; then would come the sheets for the center

staff, and so on. The last will be the Group Evaluation sheets. (Section V). Please mail these completed sheets to:

Miss M. Ann Heidbreder, Project Coordinator
Educational Media Selection Centers Project
National Book Committee, Inc.
One Park Avenue, 18th Floor
New York, New York 10016

INTERVIEW QUESTIONNAIRES

A. Center director
B. Center staff
C. Curriculum specialist
D. Classroom teacher
E. Media specialist/Librarian
F. Administrator
G. Principal

Note: <u>Each</u> team member should record
the answers to the following questions
on the colored sheets and return them
to the Project Coordinator.

Name of Interviewer: _____ Date: _____

Name of individual interviewed: _____ Title: _____

Address: _____

A. Center Director Interview

1. Who are the frequent users of this center?

   _____

   _____

   _____

2. Why do they use this center?

   _____

   _____

   _____

3. Has the center increased the competency of the user? (P) How?   [Y]   [N]

   _____

   _____

   _____

4. How many persons use this center in a typical month?   _____

   a) Is this answer an estimate? [ ]   or

   b) A count based on attendance records? [ ]

5. Describe the kind and extent of contacts with adults last week who
    were involved in:

   a) Pre-school _____

   b) Boy Scouts _____

   c) Social Service Agencies _____

   d) Other (specify) _____

6. Hours center is open:

   M   From _____ To _____
   T   From _____ To _____
   W   From _____ To _____
   Th From _____ To _____
   F   From _____ To _____
   S   From _____ To _____
   S   From _____ To _____

125

7. Estimate percent of time you spent:

   a) On administration _____ %

   b) Working with users _____ %

8. Talking about yesterday (last working day), what was your major activity?

   _____

   _____

   _____

9. Do you have a written job spec?   If yes, obtain a copy. [Y] [N]

10. What would you say are your major job responsibilities?

    _____

    _____

    _____

11. List your degree(s) or other professional training.

    _____

    _____

    _____

12. What additional professional training would you say would be beneficial to a person in your position?

    _____

    _____

    _____

13. What are the major goals of this center? (P) Any others?

    _____

    _____

    _____

14. What are the 2 or 3 major activities of this center?

    _____

    _____

    _____

15. Which one service offers the greatest contribution to advancing
    this center's educational service? Why?

    _____

    _____

    _____

16. What specific services will be offered this fall at this center?

    _____

    _____

    _____

    For each of the services mentioned, tell me why they are offered.

    _____

    _____

    _____

17. What new services are being planned within the coming year?

    _____

    _____

    _____

18. What new services would you like to see introduced?

    _____

    _____

    _____

19. What is your role in the decision to offer new services?

    _____

    _____

    _____

20. What services have been offered and discarded? Why have they been
    discarded?

    _____

    _____

    _____

21. Do you have an orientation program for users? Y N
    If yes, when offered? Describe program.

    _____

    _____

22. Is there released time for use of the center? Y N

    If yes, how many hours per month? ____hrs.

23. Does center have workshops on selection and use of media? Y N
    If yes, describe the last one offered (or the next one planned).

    _____

    _____

24. Does center have workshops on use of equipment? Y N
    If yes, describe the last one offered (or the next one planned).

    _____

    _____

25. How is the decision made to offer in-service education programs in
    the center?

    _____

    _____

26. How are new materials evaluated for the center?

    _____

    _____

27. How are new materials selected for the center?

    _____

    _____

    _____

28. What roles do users have in selection of new materials for center?

_____

_____

_____

29. When a user asks for special or individual instruction, what happens?

_____

_____

_____

30. Does center operate a mobile unit? If yes, describe.   [Y]   [N]

_____

_____

_____

31. What would you say is the best way to organize the various media in the center?

_____

_____

_____

32. Do you distribute any printed material about the center and its ser-   [Y]   [N]
vices? If yes, what? Please furnish samples if possible.

_____

_____

_____

33. Who sponsors this center?

_____

_____

_____

34. What growth plans re space exist for the center?
Next year?_____

_____

Next 5 years?_____

_____

35. What would happen if this center were abolished?

_____

_____

_____

36. Is the center given any publicity by local radio stations?   Y   N
    If yes, describe.

_____

_____

_____

37. Is the center given any publicity by local TV stations?   Y   N
    If yes, describe.

_____

_____

_____

38. Is the center given any publicity by local newspapers?   Y   N
    If yes, describe.

_____

_____

_____

39. Considering the goals and activities of this center in relation to its
    achievements how would you (as director/staff) rate this center:

    Excellent ☐   Good ☐   Fair ☐   Poor ☐

    What are the reasons for this rating?

Name of Interviewer: _____ Date: _____

Name of individual interviewed: _____ Title: _____

Address: _____

B. Center Staff Interview

1. Who are the frequent users of this center?

   _____

   _____

   _____

2. Why do they use this center?

   _____

   _____

   _____

3. Has the center increased the competency of the user? (P) How?   Y   N

   _____

   _____

   _____

4. How many persons use this center in a typical month?

   a) Is this answer an estimate? ☐   or

   b) A count based on attendance records? ☐

5. Describe the kind and extent of contacts with adults last week who were involved in:

   a) Pre-school _____

   b) Boy Scouts _____

   c) Social Service Agencies _____

   d) Other (specify) _____

6. Hours center is open:

M	From _____	To _____
T	From _____	To _____
W	From _____	To _____
Th	From _____	To _____
F	From _____	To _____
S	From _____	To _____
S	From _____	To _____

131

7. Estimate percent of time you spent:

    a) On administration   _____ %

    b) Working with users   _____ %

8. Talking about yesterday (last working day), what was your major activity?

    _____

    _____

    _____

9. Do you have a written job spec?   If yes, obtain a copy.   Y   N

10. What would you say are your major job responsibilities?

    _____

    _____

    _____

11. List your degree(s) or other professional training.

    _____

    _____

    _____

12. What additional professional training would you say would be beneficial to a person in your position?

    _____

    _____

    _____

13. What are the major goals of this center? (P) Any others?

    _____

    _____

    _____

14. What are the 2 or 3 major activities of this center?

    _____

    _____

    _____

132

15. Which one service offers the greatest contribution to advancing this center's educational service? Why?

_____

_____

_____

16. What specific services will be offered this fall at this center?

_____

_____

_____

For each of the services mentioned, tell me why they are offered.

_____

_____

_____

17. What new services are being planned within the coming year?

_____

_____

_____

18. What new services would you like to see introduced?

_____

_____

_____

19. What is your role in the decision to offer new services?

_____

_____

_____

20. What services have been offered and discarded? Why have they been discarded?

_____

_____

_____

21. Do you have an orientation program for users?
    If yes, when offered? Describe program.   [Y]   [N]

    _____

    _____

    _____

22. Is there released time for use of the center?   [Y]   [N]

    If yes, how many hours per month?   ____hrs.

23. Does center have workshops on selection and use of media?   [Y]   [N]
    If yes, describe the last one offered (or the next one planned).

    _____

    _____

    _____

24. Does center have workshops on use of equipment?   [Y]   [N]
    If yes, describe the last one offered (or the next one planned).

    _____

    _____

    _____

25. How is the decision made to offer in-service education programs in
    the center?

    _____

    _____

    _____

26. How are new materials evaluated for the center?

    _____

    _____

    _____

27. How are new materials selected for the center?

    _____

    _____

    _____

28. What roles do users have in selection of new materials for center?

_____

_____

_____

29. When a user asks for special or individual instruction, what happens?

_____

_____

_____

30. Does center operate a mobile unit? If yes, describe.   [Y]   [N]

_____

_____

_____

31. What would you say is the best way to organize the various media in
the center?

_____

_____

_____

32. Do you distribute any printed material about the center and its ser-   [Y]   [N]
vices? If yes, what? Please furnish samples if possible.

_____

_____

_____

33. Who sponsors this center?

_____

_____

_____

34. What growth plans re space exist for the center?
Next year?_____

_____

Next 5 years?_____

_____

35. What would happen if this center were abolished?

_____

_____

_____

36. Is the center given any publicity by local radio stations?   N
    If yes, describe.

_____

_____

_____

37. Is the center given any publicity by local TV stations?   Y N
    If yes, describe.

_____

_____

_____

38. Is the center given any publicity by local newspapers?   Y N
    If yes, describe.

_____

_____

_____

39. Considering the goals and activities of this center in relation to its
    achievements how would you (as director/staff) rate this center:

    Excellent ☐   Good ☐   Fair ☐   Poor ☐

    What are the reasons for this rating?

Name of Interviewer: _____ Date _____

Name of individual interviewed: _____ Title _____

Address: _____

C. <u>Curriculum Specialist Interview</u>

1. Who are the frequent users of this center?

   _____

   _____

   _____

2. Why do they use this center?

   _____

   _____

   _____

3. Has the center increased your competency? (P) How?   [Y] [N]

   _____

   _____

   _____

4. Describe the kind and extent of contacts you had with adults last week who were involved in:

   a) Pre-school _____

   b) Boy Scouts _____

   c) Social Service agencies _____

   d) Other (specify) _____

5. What are the major goals of this center? (P) Any others?

   _____

   _____

   _____

   _____

137

6. What are the 2 or 3 major activities of this center?

_____

_____

_____

7. Which one service offers the greatest contribution to advancing this center's service? Why?

_____

_____

_____

8. What specific services will be offered this fall at this center?

_____

_____

_____

9. For each of the services mentioned, tell me why they are offered.

_____

_____

_____

10. What new services would you like to see introduced?

_____

_____

_____

11. What is your role in the decision to offer new services?

_____

_____

_____

12. What services have been offered and discarded? Why have they been discarded?

_____

_____

_____

138

13. Did you ever attend an orientation program at the center? If yes, describe.

[Y]   [N]

_____

_____

_____

14. Is there released time for use of the center? If yes, how many hours per month?

_____hrs.

15. Does center have workshops on selection and use of media? If yes, describe last one attended.

[Y]   [N]

_____

_____

_____

16. Does center have workshops on use of equipment? If yes, describe last one attended.

[Y]   [N]

_____

_____

_____

17. How are new materials selected for the center?

_____

_____

_____

18. What role do users have in selection of new materials for center?

_____

_____

_____

19. When a user asks for special or individual instruction at the center what happens?

_____

_____

_____

20. What would you say is the best way to organize the various media in the center?

_____

_____

_____

21. Have you received any printed material about the center and its services? If yes, describe. [Y] [N]

_____

_____

_____

22. What would happen if this center were abolished?

_____

_____

_____

23. Who sponsors this center?

_____

_____

_____

24. Is the center given any publicity by local radio stations? If yes, describe. [Y] [N]

_____

_____

_____

25. Is the center given any publicity by local TV stations? If yes, describe. [Y] [N]

_____

_____

_____

26. Is the center given any publicity by local newspapers? If yes, describe. [Y] [N]

_____

_____

_____

27. What other direct communications do you receive from the center concerning its activities?

_____

_____

_____

28. Considering the goals and activities of this center in relation to its achievements, how would you as an educator rate this center?

Excellent ☐   Good ☐   Fair ☐   Poor ☐

What are the reasons for this rating?

_____

_____

_____

29. List your degree (s) or other professional training.

_____

_____

_____

Name of Interviewer _____ Date _____

Name of individual interviewed: _____ Title _____

Address: _____

D. Classroom Teacher Interview

1. Who are the frequent users of this center?

   _____

   _____

   _____

2. Why do they use this center?

   _____

   _____

   _____

3. Has the center increased your competency? (P) How?   [Y] [N]

   _____

   _____

   _____

4. Describe the kind and extent of contacts you had with adults last week who were involved in:

   a) Pre-school _____

   b) Boy Scouts _____

   c) Social Service agencies _____

   d) Other (specify) _____

5. What are the major goals of this center? (P) Any others?

   _____

   _____

   _____

   _____

142

6. What are the 2 or 3 major activities of this center?

_____

_____

_____

7. Which one service offers the greatest contribution to advancing this center's service? Why?

_____

_____

_____

8. What specific services will be offered this fall at this center?

_____

_____

_____

9. For each of the services mentioned, tell me why they are offered.

_____

_____

_____

10. What new services would you like to see introduced?

_____

_____

_____

11. What is your role in the decision to offer new services?

_____

_____

_____

12. What services have been offered and discarded? Why have they been discarded?

_____

_____

_____

143

13. Did you ever attend an orientation program at the center?
    If yes, describe.   Y   N

_____

_____

_____

14. Is there released time for use of the center? If yes, how many hours
    per month?   _____hrs.

15. Does center have workshops on selection and use of media? If yes,
    describe last one attended.   Y   N

_____

_____

_____

16. Does center have workshops on use of equipment? If yes, describe
    last one attended.   Y   N

_____

_____

_____

17. How are new materials selected for the center?

_____

_____

_____

18. What role do users have in selection of new materials for center?

_____

_____

_____

19. When a user asks for special or individual instruction at the
    center what happens?

_____

_____

_____

144

20. What would you say is the best way to organize the various media in the center?

_____

_____

_____

21. Have you received any printed material about the center and its services? If yes, describe.   [Y]   [N]

_____

_____

_____

22. What would happen if this center were abolished?

_____

_____

_____

23. Who sponsors this center?

_____

_____

_____

24. Is the center given any publicity by local radio stations? If yes, describe.   [Y]   [N]

_____

_____

_____

25. Is the center given any publicity by local TV stations? If yes, describe.   [Y]   [N]

_____

_____

_____

26. Is the center given any publicity by local newspapers? If yes, describe.   [Y]   [N]

_____

_____

_____

27. What other direct communications do you receive from the center concerning its activities?

_____

_____

_____

28. Considering the goals and activities of this center in relation to its achievements, how would you as an educator rate this center?

Excellent ☐   Good ☐   Fair ☐   Poor ☐

What are the reasons for this rating?

_____

_____

_____

29. List your degree (s) or other professional training.

_____

_____

_____

Name of Interviewer: _____ Date _____

Name of individual interviewed: _____ Title _____

Address: _____

E. Media Specialist/Librarian Interview

1. Who are the frequent users of this center?

   _____

   _____

   _____

2. Why do they use this center?

   _____

   _____

   _____

3. Has the center increased your competency? (P) How? $\boxed{Y}$ $\boxed{N}$

   _____

   _____

   _____

4. Describe the kind and extent of contacts you had with adults last week
   who were involved in:

   a) Pre-school _____

   b) Boy Scouts _____

   c) Social Service agencies _____

   d) Other (specify) _____

5. What are the major goals of this center? (P) Any others?

   _____

   _____

   _____

   _____

6. What are the 2 or 3 major activities of this center?

    _____

    _____

    _____

7. Which one service offers the greatest contribution to advancing
    this center's service? Why?

    _____

    _____

    _____

8. What specific services will be offered this fall at this center?

    _____

    _____

    _____

9. For each of the services mentioned, tell me why they are offered.

    _____

    _____

    _____

10. What new services would you like to see introduced?

    _____

    _____

    _____

11. What is your role in the decision to offer new services?

    _____

    _____

    _____

12. What services have been offered and discarded? Why have they been
    discarded?

    _____

    _____

    _____

148

13. Did you ever attend an orientation program at the center? If yes, describe. [Y] [N]

____

____

____

14. Is there released time for use of the center? If yes, how many hours per month? ______hrs.

15. Does center have workshops on selection and use of media? If yes, describe last one attended. [Y] [N]

____

____

____

16. Does center have workshops on use of equipment? If yes, describe last one attended. [Y] [N]

____

____

____

17. How are new materials selected for the center?

____

____

____

18. What role do users have in selection of new materials for center?

____

____

____

19. When a user asks for special or individual instruction at the center what happens?

____

____

____

20. What would you say is the best way to organize the various media in the center?

_____

_____

_____

21. Have you received any printed material about the center and its services? If yes, describe.   [Y]   [N]

_____

_____

_____

22. What would happen if this center were abolished?

_____

_____

_____

23. Who sponsors this center?

_____

_____

_____

24. Is the center given any publicity by local radio stations? If yes, describe.   [Y]   [N]

_____

_____

_____

25. Is the center given any publicity by local TV stations? If yes, describe.   [Y]   [N]

_____

_____

_____

26. Is the center given any publicity by local newspapers? If yes, describe.   [Y]   [N]

_____

_____

_____

27. What other direct communications do you receive from the center concerning its activities?

_____

_____

_____

28. Considering the goals and activities of this center in relation to its achievements, how would you as an educator rate this **center**?

Excellent ☐   Good ☐   Fair ☐   Poor ☐

What are the reasons for this rating?

_____

_____

_____

29. List your degree (s) or other professional training.

_____

_____

_____

151

Name of Interviewer: _____ Date _____

Name of individual interviewed: _____ Title:__ _____

Address: _____

F. Administrator Interview

1. Who are the frequent users of this center?

   _____

   _____

   _____

2. Why do they use this center?

   _____

   _____

   _____

3. Has the center increased your competency? (P) How?   [Y] [N]

   _____

   _____

   _____

4. Describe the kind and extent of contacts you had with adults last week
   who were involved in:

   a) Pre-school _____

   b) Boy Scouts _____

   c) Social Service agencies _____

   d) Other (specify) _____

5. What are the major goals of this center? (P) Any others?

   _____

   _____

   _____

   _____

152

6. What are the 2 or 3 major activities of this center?

_____

_____

_____

7. Which one service offers the greatest contribution to advancing
   this center's service? Why?

_____

_____

_____

8. What specific services will be offered this fall at this center?

_____

_____

_____

9. For each of the services mentioned, tell me why they are offered.

_____

_____

_____

10. What new services would you like to see introduced?

_____

_____

_____

11. What is your role in the decision to offer new services?

_____

_____

_____

12. What services have been offered and discarded? Why have they been
    discarded?

_____

_____

_____

13. Did you ever attend an orientation program at the center? ☐Y ☐N
    If yes, describe.
    _____
    _____
    _____

14. Is there released time for use of the center? If yes, how many hours
    per month?   _____hrs.

15. Does center have workshops on selection and use of media? If yes, ☐Y ☐N
    describe last one attended.
    _____
    _____
    _____

16. Does center have workshops on use of equipment? If yes, describe ☐Y ☐N
    last one attended.
    _____
    _____
    _____

17. How are new materials selected for the center?
    _____
    _____
    _____

18. What role do users have in selection of new materials for center?
    _____
    _____
    _____

19. When a user asks for special or individual instruction at the
    center what happens?
    _____
    _____
    _____

20. What would you say is the best way to organize the various media in the center?

_____

_____

_____

21. Have you received any printed material about the center and its services? If yes, describe.   [Y]   [N]

_____

_____

_____

22. What would happen if this center were abolished?

_____

_____

_____

23. Who sponsors this center?

_____

_____

_____

24. Is the center given any publicity by local radio stations? If yes, describe.   [Y]   [N]

_____

_____

_____

25. Is the center given any publicity by local TV stations? If yes, describe.   [Y]   [N]

_____

_____

_____

26. Is the center given any publicity by local newspapers? If yes, describe.   [Y]   [N]

_____

_____

_____

27. What other direct communications do you receive from the center concerning its activities?

_____

_____

_____

28. Considering the goals and activities of this center in relation to its achievements, how would you as an educator rate this **center**?

Excellent ☐   Good ☐   Fair ☐   Poor ☐

What are the reasons for this rating?

_____

_____

_____

29. List your degree (s) or other professional training.

_____

_____

_____

Name of Interviewer: _____ Date _____

Name of individual interviewed: _____ Title _____

Address: _____

G. Principal Interview

1. Who are the frequent users of this center?

   _____

   _____

   _____

2. Why do they use this center?

   _____

   _____

   _____

3. Has the center increased your competency? (P) How?   Y   N

   _____

   _____

   _____

4. Describe the kind and extent of contacts you had with adults last week
   who were involved in:

   a) Pre-school _____

   b) Boy Scouts _____

   c) Social Service agencies _____

   d) Other (specify) _____

5. What are the major goals of this center? (P) Any others?

   _____

   _____

   _____

   _____

157

6. What are the 2 or 3 major activities of this center?

_____

_____

_____

7. Which one service offers the greatest contribution to advancing this center's service? Why?

_____

_____

_____

8. What specific services will be offered this fall at this center?

_____

_____

_____

9. For each of the services mentioned, tell me why they are offered.

_____

_____

_____

10. What new services would you like to see introduced?

_____

_____

_____

11. What is your role in the decision to offer new services?

_____

_____

_____

12. What services have been offered and discarded? Why have they been discarded?

_____

_____

_____

13. Did you ever attend an orientation program at the center?
    If yes, describe.   [Y]   [N]

    _____

    _____

    _____

14. Is there released time for use of the center? If yes, how many hours
    per month?   _____hrs.

15. Does center have workshops on selection and use of media? If yes,
    describe last one attended.   [Y]   [N]

    _____

    _____

    _____

16. Does center have workshops on use of equipment? If yes, describe
    last one attended.   [Y]   [N]

    _____

    _____

    _____

17. How are new materials selected for the center?

    _____

    _____

    _____

18. What role do users have in selection of new materials for center?

    _____

    _____

    _____

19. When a user asks for special or individual instruction at the
    center what happens?

    _____

    _____

    _____

20. What would you say is the best way to organize the various media in the center?

_____

_____

_____

21. Have you received any printed material about the center and its services? If yes, describe. [Y] [N]

_____

_____

_____

22. What would happen if this center were abolished?

_____

_____

_____

23. Who sponsors this center?

_____

_____

_____

24. Is the center given any publicity by local radio stations? If yes, describe. [Y] [N]

_____

_____

_____

25. Is the center given any publicity by local TV stations? If yes, describe. [Y] [N]

_____

_____

_____

26. Is the center given any publicity by local newspapers? If yes, describe. [Y] [N]

_____

_____

_____

27. What other direct communications do you receive from the center concerning its activities?

_____

_____

_____

28. Considering the goals and activities of this center in relation to its achievements, how would you as an educator rate this **center?**

Excellent ☐   Good ☐   Fair ☐   Poor ☐

What are the reasons for this rating?

_____

_____

_____

29. List your degree (s) or other professional training.

_____

_____

_____

161

Appendix D

GROUP EVALUATION

Note: The questions in this Section are intended to elicit the impressions of the team as a whole about the center, but especially about its program. The team should attempt to evaluate the effectiveness of the activities and personnel about which more specific data have been collected on the printed questionnaires and during the individual interviews.

Center _____   Team Chairman _____

                                              Team Members _____

                                              _____

GROUP EVALUATION

The chairman will record the answer as agreed by the group but it will be his prime responsibility to obtain information from the Center Director.

1. a) What audiovisual material is most effective?

        _____

        _____

        _____

    b) What audiovisual material is poor and reason(s) why?

        _____

        _____

        _____

2. Degree to which collection is classified and catalogued?

    a) Excellent ☐   Good ☐ Fair ☐ Poor ☐

    b) Reason for group rating

        _____

        _____

        _____

3. Display of recently acquired materials?

    a) Excellent ☐   Good ☐ Fair ☐ Poor ☐

    b) Reason for group rating

        _____

        _____

        _____

163

4. a) Does center maintain an evaluation file for items
        added to the collection?   Yes ☐   No ☐

        _____

        _____

        _____

    b) How would you rate the evaluation file?

        Excellent ☐   Good ☐   Fair ☐   Poor ☐

    c) Reason for group rating

        _____

        _____

        _____

5. a) How would you rate the education programs offered
        by the center?

        Excellent ☐   Good ☐   Fair ☐   Poor ☐

    b) Reason for group rating

        _____

        _____

        _____

6. Rating of collection of: Print media and non-print
                             media

                          Excellent   Good   Fair   Poor

    a) Print media   ☐   ☐   ☐   ☐

    b) Non-print media   ☐   ☐   ☐   ☐

    c) Reason for print media rating

        _____

        _____

        _____

    d) Reason for non-print media rating

        _____

        _____

        _____

164

7. Attitude of specific person interviewed toward this Center

	Excellent	Good	Fair	Poor
Administrator	☐	☐	☐	☐
Principal	☐	☐	☐	☐
Curriculum Specialist	☐	☐	☐	☐
Media Specialist/ Librarian	☐	☐	☐	☐
Teacher	☐	☐	☐	☐
Center Staff	☐	☐	☐	☐
Director of Center	☐	☐	☐	☐
TOTAL OVERALL RATING OF CENTER	☐	☐	☐	☐

State reason(s) for overall rating.

_____

_____

_____

_____

8. Is this center more media or training centered? Cite evidence for answer

_____

_____

_____

9. What is this center's greatest strength?   Why?

_____

_____

_____

10. What is this center's greatest weakness?   Why?

_____

_____

_____

_____

165

11. To what extent does the center staff work with
    community groups? Cite examples to support answer.

    _____

    _____

    _____

12. Does this center have plans for improvement and
    change? What are they?

    _____

    _____

    _____

13. How realistic are they?

    _____

    _____

    _____

14. How realistic are indications of future financial
    support?

    a) On local level?

        _____

        _____

        _____

    b) On State level?

        _____

        _____

        _____

15. Among all persons interviewed, whom would you suggest
    we contact for further information because of the
    person's interest in and understanding of Center?

    Name _____ Title _____

    Address _____

    _____

166

16. What are the most important improvements needed by this center?

_____

_____

_____

17. Is the information about kinds and quantity of media contained on the second questionnaire reasonably accurate?

Y   N

If no, state why

_____

_____

_____

18. Is the media collection at the center adequate to support the programs being conducted?

_____

_____

_____

19. Is the necessary equipment for audiovisual media conveniently located and accessible?

_____

_____

_____

20. How would you evaluate the effectiveness of the collection in meeting the needs of the student population, i.e., is the collection relevant to their needs?

_____

_____

_____

_____

21. Is the center staff familiar and knowledgeable
     with the media collection?   Y   N

     _____

     _____

     _____

     _____

22. Is the collection balanced, i.e. are both the   balanced   ▢
     print and non-print collections good, or is one
     far superior to the other?   not balanced ▢

     _____

     _____

     _____

     _____

23. Please make additional comments about the center
     and its collection so that we can better recommend
     standards for future centers.

     _____

     _____

     _____

     _____

     _____

     _____

     _____

     _____

     _____

Appendix E

PART 1

We are having this group discussion to enrich, through your personal experiences, the data reported in the various questionnaires completed as a result of the team visits.

(Review rules, i. e. , talk one at a time, feel free to disagree, etc.)

Many of you visited more than one center, but as you are aware our letter to you designated a center that you are to represent or talk about for the purposes of this discussion. The first six questions should therefore be discussed by each of you primarily in relation to the center we designated you to represent.

la. Did your chairman brief the team by reviewing the various questionnaires before interviewing started? On your questionnaire please indicate next to la, yes or no. (If you were a team chairman did you review with your team the various questionnaires? If team chairman, next to lb on the questionnaire indicate yes or no.) Tell me about the briefing.

2a. How satisfied were you with the questionnaires that formed the basis of your interview in terms of the answers obtained? On the questionnaire next to 2a indicate your rating of the questionnaire as a basis of obtaining information .

169

2b. What would you say was the attitude of the respondent toward the interview as reflected by the answers? Next to 2b indicate your rating of his attitude.

2c. What would you say is the value of the interview you conducted? On the questionnaire next to 2c indicate your rating.

3a. Talking about your respondents, were they randomly selected by you? On the questionnaire indicate yes or no.

3b. How did you get your appointments and where were they conducted?

4a. How valuable and valid would you say was your team group evaluation? On the questionnaire next to 4a indicate your rating.

4b. Would you say the group evaluation was a team participation or primarily the role of one individual? On the questionnaire indicate whether it was team or individual.

5. Considering your background and experience, what would you say that you personally learned as a result of your visit?

6. How could this team visit have been planned to give better and more meaningful results?

The following questions relate to those of you who visited 2 or more different centers.

7. Considering the centers you visited, would you indicate the relative similarities or differences in the teams at the various centers.

8a. Considering the various centers you personally visited, will you tell me whether in your opinion these centers differed, and also the reasons for the differences if they exist.

8b. If you were forced to make a value judgment, and considering the centers you visited, which center in your opinion was better than the other center or centers.

8c. Talking about the training function of a Media Center, what types of training take place at the Center(s) you visited?

PART 2

9. Phase 2 will concentrate on developing guidelines for improving existing centers and helping those who wish to set up new centers. Assuming a set of guidelines might best be organized by having a number of major parts or divisions, if you were to organize a set of guidelines what major divisions would you suggest? Before discussing, would you list, next to 9 on your questionnaire, the major divisions you suggest.

10. . Would you select one major division that should be included in the guidelines and for it list five of the most important guideline items for that division. Before discussing enter next to number 10 on your questionnaire.

QUESTIONNAIRE

1a.   Yes ☐   No ☐

1b.   Yes ☐   No ☐

2a.   Excellent ☐   Good ☐   Fair ☐   Poor ☐

2b.   Excellent ☐   Good ☐   Fair ☐   Poor ☐

2c.   Excellent ☐   Good ☐   Fair ☐   Poor ☐

3a.   Yes ☐   No ☐

4a.   Excellent ☐   Good ☐   Fair ☐   Poor ☐

4b.   Team ☐   Individual ☐

9.   _____

       _____

       _____

       _____

       _____

       _____

       _____

       _____

       _____

10. _____

_____

_____

_____

_____

_____

_____

Name_____ Affiliation _____

Team Member ☐   Team Chairman ☐

Center Represented   _____

Additional Centers   _____
   Visited
                      _____

173

**Educational
Media
Selection
Centers
Program**

A nationwide survey and demonstration
program in four phases to help develop
facilities, procedures, and programs for
the integrated and effective use of all
media resources by educators and other
adults.

SCOPE & PURPOSE

Experienced, critical examination of instructional materials is imperative for improving the selection process.

Ideally, an educational media selection center serves adults—teachers, librarians and others—who are responsible for educating the young. The center provides a wide range of materials, both print and non-print, for examination and preview prior to selection and purchase for use with children and youth. The center is staffed by professional media specialists who assist in selecting and evaluating materials, and who train others to do so. The center also has the capability to be the site of flexible, continuing inservice programs of training in the *use* of media in education.

Fostering such centers is the purpose of the Educational Media Selection Centers Program. It encompasses a seven-year study in four successive phases, and is administered by the National Book Committee with a grant from the U.S. Office of Education.

The results of the EMSC Program should encourage a high degree of integrated media services in all instructional programs.

Phase I   (June 1968—Jan. 1970):

. . .*identification, study and evaluation of existing centers (or components of such centers)*. . .questionnaires (about 2220) were sent to all identifiable centers and, on the basis of information received, 440 were followed up by a more comprehensive questionnaire. After analysis, about 50 centers which seemed to offer components of an effective program were studied further through on-site visits by professionally qualified surveyor-teams of two or three educators and media specialists. Simultaneously, the original Executive Advisory Council for the project was enlarged, becoming the EMSC Advisory Committee, which includes official representatives of more than 40 national education and library organizations.

The information collected by the survey teams has been evaluated and assembled into an analytical report, with a summary of the findings. The larger representational Advisory Committee reviewed the report before its submission and subsequent approval by the U.S. Office of Education. (Educational Media Selection Centers: Identification and Analysis of Current Practices, published by American Library Association; Fall, 1970)

Phase II   (May 1970—May 1971):

. . .*preparation and publication of guidelines for establishing or improving centers.*. . the development of these guidelines will provide blueprints for educational agencies that plan to upgrade and extend their collections and services and for those administrators who are planning new centers.

Phase III   (at least 3 years):

. . .*establishment and operation of demonstration centers reflecting a variety of administrative and service patterns.*. . based on the guidelines, a variety of models—or demonstration educational media selection centers—will be established. Some existing facilities will be expanded into comprehensive educational media selection centers. The establishment of new centers would be called for only when absolutely necessary. All centers would be fully functional while serving as models.

Phase IV   (approx. 2 years):

. . .*evaluation of the model centers and guidelines, and dissemination of information about the program.*. . a book based on comprehensive evaluations of both the Phase III model centers and the Phase II guidelines will be written and published during Phase IV. A film about programs and services of educational media selection centers also will be produced, accompanied by a discussion and study guide. Simultaneously, a broad program of public information about the project will be carried out.

175

Funded (Phases I & II) by Library and Information Sciences Research Branch, National Center for Educational Research and Development, United States Office of Education

Administered
by
The National Book Committee, Inc.
One Park Avenue
New York, N.Y. 10016

ADVISORY COMMITTEE

176

Dorothy M. McGeoch, American Association
of Colleges for Teacher Education

Philip J. McNiff, Association of College and
Research Libraries

A. Edward Miller, President, Berlitz Publications, Inc., and former President of Alfred
Politz Research, Inc.

Andrew J. Mitchell, Department of Elementary School Principals

Dr. Merle M. Ohlsen, American Personnel and
Guidance Association

Dr. Franklin Patterson, President, Hampshire
College

Cary Potter, National Association of Independent Schools

John Rowell, School of Library Science, Case
Western Reserve University

Arnold W. Salisbury, American Association of
School Administrators

Erma R. Schell, Association of Classroom
Teachers

David Selden, American Federation of Teachers

David Shaw, American Institute of Architects

Sister Helen Sheehan, Catholic Library Association

Dr. Elizabeth A. Simendinger, National Science Teachers Association

Gerald E. Sroufe, National Committee for
Support of the Public Schools

Gordon I. Swanson, The Rural Education
Association

Harold W. Tucker, Director, Queens Borough
Public Library

Robert Verrone, Children's Book Council

Theodore Waller, President, Grolier Educational Corporation

Nell White, National Education Association

Roger Yarrington, American Association of
Junior Colleges

Staff

Program Director

Cora Paul Bomar, Assistant Prof., School of
Education, University of North Carolina at
Greensboro

Program Coordinator

M. Ann Heidbreder, Staff Associate, National
Book Committee, Inc.

Administrative Assistant

Wanda R. Koskinen

~ ~ ~

*Founded in 1954 as a nonprofit
organization, the National Book Committee is composed of prominent private
citizens associated with the arts and
sciences, education, communications,
the professions, and the business community. It sponsors the National Library
Week Program in cooperation with the
American Library Association, the National Medal for Literature, administers
the National Book Awards, and conducts
research in a variety of fields related to
reading and library development.*

~ ~ ~

**Inquiries about the project should be directed
to:**

**Educational Media Selection Centers Program
National Book Committee, Inc.:
One Park Avenue
New York, N.Y. 10016**

177

"In a September 24 briefing on the project, Dr. Mason Gross . . . said: 'Our educational community is confronted by a complicated problem of epidemic proportions: a vast and varied student body. . .and a rapidly increasing tide of interdisciplinary materials in all media, new subject matter and techniques. . . .Learning and teaching are such individual processes, involving delicate balances of experience, selection, and response. If through this project we can demonstrate a variety of ways to put the best educational resources, ideas, and innovations within reach of students, their teachers, and librarians, we will have made a valid contribution toward solving some of the most urgent problems of education.' "

School Library Journal, October 15, 1968

~ ~ ~

"Because of the staggering amounts of instructional materials (books, films, filmstrips, and other instructional aids), teachers, school librarians, curriculum analysts, and media specialists today find it difficult to select new materials from catalogs.

"These educators need central locations where they can examine and get information about available materials. Fostering such centers is the aim of a project of the National Book Committee. The step into multiple kinds of media marks a departure from its previous exclusive focus on books."

Scholastic Teacher, October 18, 1968

~ ~ ~

"The project's purpose is to make available (knowledge of) the finest educational resources, ideas, and innovations for students, teachers, and librarians."

Audiovisual Instruction, November, 1968

GPO 887-89 1